Laughter, Sweat & Fears

Life in the Factory

"A humorous look at over thirty years of life inside a factory environment."

By

Trevor Whitehead

I dedicate this book to the hundreds if not thousands of people I crossed paths with throughout my time at the factory.

Geoffrey Martin-Smith, for his help in reminding me of some of the characters and comical moments we encountered.

Warren Gibson, for revealing the real reason for the sudden departure of a certain convenor.

Roy Burton for his help in confirming the names of certain security personnel.

Last but not least, Gordon Beattie, Steve Battle, Steve Beavis, Mark Clothier, the late Brian Crease, Rob Fellows, Neil Fullam, John Levy, Mark Lewin, John Manning and Terry Watts. I have the fondest of memories with you guys.

A note from the author:

I wasn't quite sure how to attempt this book. I've been quite successful writing four humorous, followed by an attempt at a crime book. I was worried that a book about a manufacturing plant would only appeal to the people connected to the place. But on reflection I thought anybody who has worked in a factory atmosphere can identify and enjoy reading about the ups and downs of factory life. My first book "The Curry Affect," was 50% true and 50% fiction. It's loosely based on my experiences living in a shared house in my early twenties.
So, in the end I felt the best approach would be to follow that familiar route again, but this time covering my working life at the factory, from the mid 1970's through to 2010. I will try and keep it in some form of chronicle order, however, at times, this may not always be possible. I will also venture away from the factory to my life outside and my involvement with the Labour Party and Trade Union activities. I will try and keep it as accurate and humorous as I can. My aim is to make it a fun read.
I will use nicknames when I think fit, real names when appropriate and false names to protect a few from vigilantes. All that you read are based on true events, there is going to be no fiction in this book. If certain individuals are not happy that they come across in a bad light, well, what can I say? I'm not sorry. Certain

people made my time at the plant, let's just say, uncomfortable.

For me, my working life at the factory was one hell of a journey. I met literally thousands of people over thirty plus years. Many of these characters will feature in this book. It's funny because I literally knew hundreds of people there, some for donkey years, but didn't know them by their name.

My father worked at the factory right from the beginning in the early sixties. He was transferred down from Dagenham. He once told me when he started there he could see from one corner at the back of the building to a corner at the front. Before a single machine was in place. Well, all of us who have been inside the Factory know that's a huge area. The place is the size of a mini town. The days before Health and Safety went OTT, people used to get around on pushbikes. I can remember when I started and watched in amazement as a single engine block would eventually be driven off the end of the assembly line an all singing and dancing tractor. That block had all the necessary parts added to it. Crankshaft, pistons, camshaft and all the other parts that eventually made it a fully working engine. Then moved over to the assembly line where over a period of a couple of days of weaving up and down the lines, the tractor was slowly put together. It was some feat I can tell you, and at one point we were building well in excess of a hundred tractors a day.

Not quite as long as Coronation Street, the factory has provided employment for many. Through all the plant's ups and downs, I loved working there. I will never speak badly of the place. It's still churning out tractors to this day, well over fifty years now. Something I and many others should be proud to have been a part of.

The factory has a great reputation for building a quality product. That's why it's survived for so many years. Long may it continue.

"A little taster."

You know, in every factory you'll find a village idiot. Well in my time as a trade union representative, I came across two. One is now retired, but he'll feature later in this book. The other I believe is now a prominent figure in the trade union side at the plant. As he is still working there it's only fair I protect his identity. So, let's call him "The Munch."

Now, for some unknown reason, the "Munch" became the factory's union, health and safety representative. When I found out about this appointment I thought the convenor at the time had lost his marbles? Not one of your better moments, Geoff? (Ex Convenor)

However, the "Munch" if anything, was enthusiastic and to be fair to the guy tried his best.

Now, this comical encounter I can remember as if it was yesterday. There had been a near-miss accident on the final assembly line. If my memory serves me correctly I believe a rear wheel had come off one of the tow tractor trailers that supplied the final assembly, this resulted in a slightly grazed assembly worker. Admittedly it could have been nasty, luckily the guy involved was quick on his feet and managed to dodge the bullet.

So, in the aftermath of this incident, the "Munch" called all the stewards in for a meeting. When I say all the stewards, we were down to a handful by then. I don't know what it was, maybe I had a touch of wind. But I walked into the meeting smiling. Now, one thing that always went against the "Munch."

He came from Bristol. So, he spoke with a broad West Country accent that to the Essex man, well, not to put a too finer point on it, sounds thick.
The "Munch" took one look at me and pointed.
'This is no laughing matter, Trevor. That man could have been killed!! Worst still, he could have broken a leg!!'
Just a taster of what's to come.

Enjoy the book.

Chapter 1

The early years.

I guess my first memories of the factory date back to the late sixties. I must have been around twelve at the time. We were living in a tiny village called Stow Maries, you know, one of those blink and you'll miss it type places. My dad had completed twenty-five years with the company and was going on a night out to London's Talk of the Town. When I think back, my dad would only have been thirty-nine, he started work at fourteen. Now, these were the days before you could take your wife to the long service dinners. We lived down a small lane and I remember standing next to my mum as this big coach manoeuvred along our lane and pulled up outside our bungalow. Dad, in his best suit, climbed aboard and we waved him off. Next morning, I woke up and could smell vomit. Walking in the kitchen, mum was clearing up the aftermath of the boozy night out. Sat on the kitchen table was a vomit-stained Engelbert Humperdinck LP. Signed by the man himself. My dad had it framed, and for years that vomit stained LP hung on the wall. Not long after that, my granddad passed away, on my mum's side. My nan gave my dad, granddad's old moped. It was one of those 49cc pedal to start types. Now, Stow Maries was a good thirteen miles away from the factory, doesn't sound a lot, but on a moped that had a top speed of about twenty miles an hour, it was far enough. I'm guessing it did a lot of miles to the gallon, so that was enough to get dad peddling. I remember the afternoon we had really bad snow, dad had rung and said it was bad at work. He left work early but unbeknown to mum and me, the moped wouldn't start. So, he peddled home the thirteen miles. Bad enough on a normal bike, on a moped it must have been a killer. He arrived home about three hours later, dripping wet and knackered. I think after that the romance of the moped died. Back to driving his Vauxhall Viva.

My dad was a bit of a terror at work, I don't have to look far to find where I get my mischievous nature from. He was a tinsmith at the plant, a highly skilled trade. I used to watch in awe at some of the things he made from sheet metal. I wouldn't imagine there are many of his creations left in the plant now. He made many of the guards and like for engine machining, sadly that side of the factory has long gone. In my early years working there, I used to have my tea break with him. Now a small fact, never argue with your dad, he's always right. The classic example, sugar! My dad never took sugar in his tea. I used to take three. He'd make me a cuppa, then I'd have to go to one of his mates and scrounge the sugar. He said if you can drink tea with no sugar for one week, you'll never take sugar again. So, for a week I suffered, I was a bit of a teapot, so maybe six to eight cups a day. After a week, I made a cup and put three sugars in, and as dad predicated, I couldn't drink it. I sat with him one tea break and it must have been around November time. I say this with confidence because all of a sudden, he stood up and pulled this huge firework out of his bag.

'Loudest banger on the market,' he informed me.

The other two tinsmiths, Ernie and Bob came over and inspected the firework. Now unbeknown to me, the tinsmiths were in dispute with a certain General Foreman, who so happened had his office right next to the tinsmith's area of work. My dad proceeded to light the banger and throw it on the roof of the office. You can imagine the noise as it went off on the metal roof. The foreman ran out with the clerk who worked in the office with him. I can see him now, tea dripping from his shirt throwing a right tantrum at my dad.

For the life of me I can't remember General foreman's name, if it comes to me I'll put it in. (Sid Miller, I think) The clerk I can remember, let's call him Moody, he will feature at a later date. He and my dad put a joint suggestion in once and won a new car between them. My dad was a compulsive suggestion scheme contributor. He'd stick an idea in at least once a week. He used the phrase "got to be in it to win it" thirty years before the lottery slogan came out. I think the suggestion scheme died when we were taken over by another company.

For some reason, my dad always went to work in a collar and tie and carried a briefcase. A bit over the top to carry cheese sandwiches? I never asked him why,? Thinking back now I'm assuming it was to impress the neighbours.

He had some strange habits. When I started at the factory I had people coming up to me saying, "Your George Whitehead's son, aren't you?"
My dad's name was Edward, mum called him Ted. So not sure where this other name came from. But at work, everybody called him George. A few memories always come to mind when I think of my late father. The first one was when I got myself chucked off the school bus for fighting. I'm ashamed to admit I was a bit of a handful at school, I would take anyone on, and if they were bigger, I'd tool up with my sister's rounders bat, well that was until it was confiscated. This particular day I had a set too with a lad called Michael Friend. A real gobshite with a big mouth. Things came to a head on the journey home from school one day. The driver stopped the coach and chucked us out in the middle of nowhere. Deciding to be clever, I thought the quickest way to get home was a straight line. So, I headed through fields and all sorts. My dad had come out in the car to look for me, so he wasn't best pleased when he saw me walking up the lane, covered in mud. My mum went mad at me and sent me to bed without any tea. Bless my dad, he sneaked in a while later with a sandwich for me. So, next day I thought no more of it. The afternoon's journey home all seemed normal. No fighting, well I couldn't face another night without chips. The school bus used to drop me off in a pub car park. The pub was called the Stow Bullocks. Unfortunately, a few years later it closed and is now a private residence. As the bus pulled into the car park

I could see my dad's car parked up. As I stepped off the bus my dad appeared.
'Wait in the car,' he instructed me. Now what I should have mentioned, we Whitehead's are a solid breed. My dad was over six feet and had arms the size of an average man's legs. His brother, my uncle Barry is a colossus of a man. Six feet-six, and not the type you'd want to mess with. As I reached the car and looked around I could see my dad pummeling the bus driver. Let's just say I never had to walk home again.

Angel Delight. My god, I could never eat one of those again. My dad came home from work one day and marched in carrying a huge box containing the popular dessert, Angel Delight. There had been an accident on his way home from work
and loads of these boxes had been scattered about. Dad being dad, had one away. Now, to begin with, I loved them, each night after dinner, mum would pop out a bowl of the chocolate dessert, and I mean each night. I never counted how many boxes were packed into the huge box, but after about a year I couldn't face another one. Now, I'm a chocoholic, but even to this day, I couldn't face a chocolate Angel Delight.

The Pig. No, I'm not talking about someone at work. I'm talking about the pig my dad knocked down on the way to work. We were living in Maldon when this happened. Occasionally my dad and I would travel to work together. My dad would never buy a car with the company discount voucher. He loved the Datsun.

Would change it every couple of years. So, this particular morning we're on our way to work, I wasn't taking particular attention to the road ahead when my dad suddenly hit the brakes as out of nowhere came this pig. Bang, he hit the front of the car with a hell of a thud. We were on a country road, early morning, no one about, the pig was dead, so, we somehow managed to stick him in the back of my dad's hatchback. We had a real struggle trying to lift it in I can tell you.

'What on earth you going to do with it?' I asked.

'Making bacon,' my dad replied. Unfortunately for us, ten minutes up the road, a grunting sound signalled that the pig had come back to life. Trust me when I tell you, he was one unhappy pig. The next five minutes were spent trying to get it out of the car. Eventually, with some sheer pulling and pushing, we got it out. The pig ran off, last seen heading towards Wickford High Street. The interior of my dad's car, absolutely wrecked. Cost him a lot of money to put it right. Just to wind him up, I sent him over a couple of bacon rolls for his morning tea break. Later that morning I was called over by a Wickford guy by the name of Peter Bell.

'Here, Trevor, never guess what I saw this morning on my way to work.'

'A pig?'

'How'd you know?'

'We gave him a lift, dropped him off near the High Street, lived in a right pigsty.'

I can only remember dad being really upset with me once. Not because of what I'd done, but because I was plastered all over the front page of our local paper "The Maldon & Burnham Standard" for two weeks. I say two weeks because it was a weekly newspaper.

I used to go to a youth club in a little village not far from Maldon, a village called Cock Clarkes. My girlfriend at the time lived there. We used to go to the village hall on a Wednesday night, meet friends and basically it was just a hanging out place. I had just turned seventeen, still riding about on my scooter, but taking driving lessons. We went one night and were informed that it was the last time the youth club would be open. Shock horror! Turned out a man who lived opposite kept complaining to the council about the noise and mess. So, I hatched a plan to teach this man a lesson, I was out to get revenge. Now, with a couple of mates, we decided how funny it would be if we placed a pretend bomb on this guy's doorstep. So, over the next couple of evenings, in my dad's shed, the three of us built what we thought a bomb would look like. I can still see the finished article now. One of those big square type 9-volt batteries, three plastic toilet roll holders, painted to look like TNT. Putty, wires going from the battery into the putty. An alarm clock and all finished off by making a plinth for it to sit on. The three of us stood back and admired our work. So off to Cock Clarkes that evening. The homemade bomb placed on his doorstep, covered by a cardboard box. I walked over to the phone box, found his number, and rang him.

'Hello.'
'Listen arsehole, I'll teach you to get our youth club closed. Open your front door, I've left you a present.'
With that, the three of us scarpered. At 3 am, there is a banging on my mum and dad's front door. I could see the blue flashing light reflecting on my bedroom ceiling. I heard my dad thumping down the stairs and utter the words most dads would say after a policeman asked if I lived there.
'He's been in all night.'
Needless to say, the shit had hit the fan. We'd made the phoney bomb look too real. The police wouldn't touch it, they called in the bomb disposal unit. I think it was safe to say, they weren't happy. Our timing was bad because of the troubles linked to the IRA, which had been going for a couple of years by then.
It went to court and because I made the phone call, I was labelled as the ringleader. What didn't help was I was seventeen and the other two were still sixteen. So, the papers could only print my name. We went to court on a Wednesday. Because the local paper had a cut-off time for printing, I was on the front page, a photo of me arriving in court, and those famous words at the end of the article .... "Case continues."
I ended up on probation for a year. The paper picked up the story the following week. I think my mum got the brunt of, "I saw your Trevor in the paper." She served in some little High Street bakers. When mum was unhappy, dad was unhappy. I think it's fair to say life was a bit fragile in the Whitehead household for a few weeks after that.

I guess through my teenage years I gave him some eye-rolling moments, but he let me learn by my own mistakes. I can only ever remember him giving me one piece of advice.
'Never go out with a girl with big hands?'

So, let's get back to the factory. It was a time when you could get anything. There was always somebody selling something. I heard a rumour that a man walked around carrying a clipboard for years selling insurance. Apparently, he didn't even work for the company! Football pools collected on a Thursday. Oily Joe, fork truck driver out of the stores. He must have made a killing collecting the football pools in the plant. I was working for Central Maintenance. A wide range of skills and ages, at the time I was one of the youngest. I was a Labour Party man, even back then, and took a keen interest in the Trade Union. Now, my first Shop Steward was an Irishman named Peter Maloney. Stout, cloth cap and a roll up permanently hanging from his lip. I had a lot of time for Peter, if you've ever seen the classic film, "I'm alright Jack," starring Peter Sellars as the Trade Union leader "Fred Kite." I think a lot of "Fred Kite" was in Peter. Unfortunately, we had a new manager arrive, a fly by night character by the name of, Gerry Bomando. A fiery character, who looked like an aging gigolo. Fat, with his shirt tucked into his trousers. Smelt of cheap aftershave and very quickly put an end to Peter's reign. Basically, Peter took him on and got his arse smacked. He was no match for this new man, and it came to a head when Bomando ridiculed Peter in front of many of us. Bomando came in and tried to make a name for himself by making Central Maintenance huge. It seemed every time I came off a week of nights and on to the day shift, they'd be three or four new faces. Of course, in the end, I think our budget was well over, so in an attempt to pull it back he slashed all overtime. Peter tried to reason with him, but Bomando wasn't having any of it. Respect for Peter dwindled and soon the Shop Stewards election came. Peter was finished, and after the ballot up stepped Bobby Graham.

Now, there was a character who could bamboozle everybody. Now, Bobby Graham was a stocky little Irishman with a fearful reputation. I'd heard many a story of his exploits at the Irish club. I can picture him now, five feet four, grey greased back hair. Now Bobby had one particular flaw, no one could understand him. It was a trait that got worse if he got excited. Now wanting to make an early name for himself as our union rep, he had a public clash with Bomando. He launched an attack on the manager. Unfortunately, none of us, including Bomando didn't understand what the hell he was ranting about. It was around this time that I knew I wanted to be the Shop Steward. The only thing I had against me was my youth, Peter Maloney and Bobby Graham must have been around the fifty plus mark at that time. First thing I had to do was belittle Bobby Graham, followed by a stand against Bomando, I needed to show the lads I wasn't scared to speak up.

So, when Bobby had a stand up with Bomando, it was time to step forward. So, after Bobby had scathed

Bomando, I knew what would come next, I'd seen and heard it before. Bomando who loved to play to an audience would hold his arms out and say 'I haven't a clue what you're on about, Bobby?'
'He said you're a c***.' Both looked around at me.
'No, he didn't.'
'Yes, he did, he said you're a c*** and a useless prick. If you don't start dishing out the overtime he's going to knock you out.' With that statement I walked off leaving them to it, my reputation had started to rocket.

We suffered Bobby for a few more weeks until things started to get ugly. Nothing worse than men not getting any overtime. We'd not been back at work long after a strike, so we were keen to try and recover the lost money. Bomando wouldn't budge, something had to give. I'd personally had my fill with Bobby, I had a set to with him one day, he still was sulking over my translation moment with him and Bomando. I didn't know if this confrontation was going to lead to blows, he was at least eight inches shorter than me and I must have been four stone heavier. Plus, he was giving away about thirty years. I tried my best to hide my fear and stand my ground expecting the worse, but after another rant, he stormed off. He didn't know it at the time, but it was over for him. We needed a steward that we could understand, someone with a bit more brain as well as brawn. I did a petition for a vote of no confidence in Bobby. Show's what his reputation was like when a few colleagues were scared to sign. Luckily, we had enough people sign to force another Shop Steward Election. Cometh the moment, cometh the man. I was voted in and became a Shop Steward at twenty-two.

Now, someone was looking down on me, because within a week of me becoming the Shop Steward for Central Maintenance, Bomando was gone. At last the hierarchy had seen through the then managers ridiculous way of running a maintenance department. Of course, I did what any Shop Steward would do, I put a rumour out that I'd been to see the Plant Manager to get Bomando removed. For a while, I was the best thing since sliced bread. Still wet behind the ears, I was brash and cocky. Little did I know this would lead to my first of many showdowns with the Plant Convenor at that time. My first encounter was with the fearful *Bill Cleary* didn't go well. In fact, it was nearly all over before it started.

Chapter 2

The Union in its heyday.

In the late nineteen-seventies, the trade unions were at their peak. These were the days of walkouts, long strikes, big pay rises. I've been on a nine-week strike, and let me tell you, it was harsh. Although finding work was quite easy back then. It became a shock to the system to do real manual work. I found an advert for a hod carrier, cash in hand. Eleven pounds a day, it was more than I was getting paid working at the factory. I did my usual, I can do that and applied for the position.

'You done hod work before?' The guy in charge looked at me suspiciously.

'Of course, I have.' I thought how hard can carrying a few bricks and a bit of cement be?

'Okay, start tomorrow at eight.' I went home, stopped on the way and bought a hod from ironmongers and a broom handle. Next morning, I turned up at the building site, take the hod out of the boot of my mark 2 Cortina and march over to the guy who hired me. His welcome left a bit to be desired.

'C***.'

Not sure if this was the usual welcome for a new guy, so I just smiled.

'What you got there?' He pointed to my sparkling brand new hod.

'Well it's not a nine iron, is it?' This remark caused a repeat of his welcome.

He grabbed my hod and walked over and sawed at least two-thirds of the handle off. I felt a right cock. To be fair after a shaky start, I got the hang of things. Bloody hard work I can tell you. I had two brickie's to keep up with. Bricks and mortar. I somehow managed it to the end of the week and picked a cheque up for fifty-five pounds. That was enough encouragement for me to turn up the following week. I kept thinking, "It's only for a few more days." The company being on strike was big news and each evening on the TV it looked like the strike would soon be over. The hell it was. Nine long weeks. At one point, I did consider taking up the hod full-time, fifty-five quid for four and a half days work was tempting. However, I had started in the middle of September, come late November it was a different ball game. Cold and wet, hard graft, any thoughts of a change of career soon disappeared. We'd been on strike seven weeks when on the news my dad and I thought it was over. We'd been offered a 17% pay rise. Dad went to the mass meeting as I was still working on the building site. As I drove home that night and listened to the news on the radio, I couldn't believe the offer had been turned down? It was done on a show of hands, my dad said there was a near riot when after the vote the convenor stood on a back of a Transit and said the voters rejected the deal. By all accounts, the vote was two to one in favour of acceptance. However, the union asked for a rejection and no way was Bill Cleary going to look a fool by accepting the deal. So, another two weeks went by and we finally accepted a rise of 23%. The days of a hands shown vote would shortly disappear.

A couple of years later we were on strike again. Not fancying bringing the hod out of retirement, I saw an advert for delivery drivers at the Corona depot in Chelmsford. I went for an interview and told them the truth. Well, not all the truth obviously, I didn't mention I was already employed. I spun a tale about wanting to try the job out for a month to see if it was for me. I said I could only work cash in hand for the month. They must have been desperate because they offered me eight pounds a day cash in hand. Not very good money, but when you're on six pounds a week strike pay, trust me, it felt like a fortune.
So, my first morning I turn up. The delivery trucks you could drive with a normal driving licence. This so-called depot supervisor threw me a book with the day's deliveries. He told me it's up to me to load the truck and find the delivery addresses. It's funny, as I think back I now realise where some of my characters in my first book have come from. This depot supervisor didn't like me and was the most unhelpful person I've met.
In other circumstances I think I would have had a set too with this little shit, but I need the work so let it go. I checked how much stock I needed, and I start loading up all different types of the then famous fizzy drink. Now here's the thing, the first morning I loaded what I needed, I drive to the gate and the security guard waved me through. Now whether this guard eventually got the job at Heathrow looking

after Brink's – Mat gold bullion, I can't possibly comment. He never checked a thing. Well, me being the type not to look a gift horse in the mouth took advantage over the following few weeks. I'm not going to hang myself, but you can imagine what went on. In a way, I was sad when the strike was over, as were my family and friends.

The convenor, Bill Cleary ran the stewards with an iron fist. He didn't suffer fools gladly. I can't remember how many Shop Stewards there were at that time, over thirty at the time. The *rat*, who would eventually become convenor, was also fearful of Bill, as were most of the stewards. Being a member of the Labour Party was compulsory, as was attending a monthly branch meeting outside of the plant.
My first Shop Stewards meeting was an eye opener in many ways. I decided my best policy was to keep quiet, watch and learn I thought.
Now I didn't know a lot of the stewards, but one I did know was a guy called Roy. His surname escapes me, he worked in the lab. Nice guy, always pleasant. He was the union rep looking after the canteen. A job I fancied as he got a free breakfast and lunch each day. No wonder he was beginning to resemble Billy Bunter. Anyway, Roy announced he'd made an agreement with the canteen management to have piped music in the canteen. Roy sat there all smug, thinking he'd done a good thing, as did I.
However, Bill decided to bring him down a peg or two.

'How dare you agree to something like this without bringing it back to the stewards. We are the ones who will say yes or no to piped music. Now get up and go and tell the canteen management that you have overstepped your position. Don't you ever agree to anything until you bring it here, to the table.'
Poor Roy, he sat there glassy-eyed for a minute, then stood up and left the meeting. Not only had he been well and truly bollocked, it had been done with all the stewards present. A lesson learned.
The meeting continued until Bill decided to flex his muscles towards me. After a gentle introduction to the other stewards, I thought the meeting would be a breeze. So, when Bill turned on me I was a bit surprised and unprepared, to say the least.
'I have to say, Trevor, I don't like these votes of no confidence in a Shop Steward. If there was a problem with Bobby Graham, you could have spoken to me.'
Now having witnessed poor Roy's humiliation, I decided attack was the best form of defence. Of course, being green behind the ears I didn't think of the consequences.
'Sorry Bill, but when a manager has the steward in his pocket, it's time for action. I don't give a fuck if you don't like a vote of no confidence, it had to be done. No way was we prepared to have another two years with a steward we needed a translator to understand.' I sat down and nothing more was said. However, I'd blotted my copy book and I think it's fair to say my stint as a shop steward wouldn't last long while Bill Cleary remained the convenor. I missed out on all the trips and basically was given the cold

shoulder. I never knew the reason behind Bill's departure. One minute he was there, then he was gone. For some reason in the back of my mind, I have a feeling he did surface a few years later. Something to do with dodgy diet pills if my memory serves me correct.

I'll pick up the convenor story later in the book.

Those early years I had some good foreman. Alf Nicolson comes to mind. What a storyteller, he'd hold Council many a night and give us some navy stories. However, the other foreman Johnny Teague was an utter cock in my opinion. He didn't like me and was constantly on my back. But, just like Bomando, I saw him off. Little did I know what was coming. The worst kind of foreman is an ex-shop steward. Step forward, Jimmy Ferris.
When I first started at the plant, Jimmy Ferris was a Vehicle Repair fitter and a Shop Steward. When I eventually started doing night work it was a known joke that if a vehicle went down after midnight, it would have to wait for the day shift to repair. The foreman wouldn't wake him *allegedly.*
So, one Monday morning I walked in and saw him prancing about in a shirt and tie, I knew things were about to get worse. The early weeks he'd run around like a blue arse fly trying to impress. We had a running battle for a number of years. It was around this time that I discovered I could impersonate our top maintenance manager at the time, Albert Musto. Oh, I had some fun on the phone taking him off. I

could see Ferris in the office just about to have his lunch, I had just done a repair job, but was going to log it off after my lunch. So, I walked next door to the heat treatment department and used their phone. The Moody answered and in my gruffest Musto voice, I barked.

'Put Ferris on.' I could hear Moody whispering, 'It's Albert.'

'Yes sir,' Christ I nearly gave the game away on hearing Ferris grovel.

'Listen Ferris, this job, so and so.' I spoke about the repair I'd done.

'If it's not completed in the next ten minutes you'll find yourself back on hourly pay putting the wheels on the tractors.'

'Don't you worry sir, I'll get straight on it.' The phone went dead. I walked back out onto the aisle just as Ferris came running out.

'Whitehead,' he shouted. I pretended I didn't hear and kept walking.

'Whitehead,' he screamed a second time. I stopped and shouted that I was just about to go to the canteen. He came running over.

'This job you're on. How are you getting on?'

'I've just this second finished it.' I could see the wave of relief come over him.

'That's good. I've just had Albert on the phone chasing me up about it. But I told him, don't you go worrying my boys, Albert. It will be repaired when it's repaired.' What a Bullshitter.

Moody said something sarcastic to me one day, so I thought you can have some Musto treatment too.

I phoned the office near lunch time.
'Hello Moody, it's Albert.'
'Hello Albert, what can I do for you?'
'I tell you what you can do for me, go over to the canteen and eat my steak dinner.'
'What?'
'I ordered a nice steak lunch, but my gout is playing up. The doctor told me to lay off the steak.'
'I thought it was chicken that did that?'
'No, it's steak that does it to me. Anyway, Jim Ferris told me how well you've been running things in the office, so have the steak as a thank you.'
'Well, if you're sure Albert.'
'Of course, I'm sure. Get yourself over to the canteen now. Tell the chef you've come to eat Albert's steak.'
I hung up, as I walked towards the office he came bounding out.
'Enjoy your sandwiches, I'm just going for a nice steak.' I watched him flounce off. Sucker.
These phone calls became a welcome outlet, but unfortunately, all good things come to an end. Albert Musto retired and in stepped Les Clemmie. Now, Clemmie was a man of few words, I don't think I heard a word from him for about five years, this put an end to my impersonations .... For a while, at least. This caused a reshuffle of maintenance staff. It was decided to put us on a 3-shift system. Now the extra money was welcome, but it was the most unsociable type of shift work. 7am-3pm, 3pm-11pm, 11pm to 7am. Friday's were the worst; Friday late shift and Friday nights were a killer. Along with this announcement came a promotion for Jim Ferris, he

was now our general Foreman. I couldn't believe it, but at least that would keep him away from me, or so I thought. A foreman was brought in for each shift. On one shift came the Irishman *Tony Lynch*. Now Tony will feature later on in the book. If you can imagine the Irish comedian Dave Allan, he was a lot like him. Had the Irish dry sense of humour, and wouldn't take any nonsense from anybody, including Jim Ferris. The next shift had a guy called *Ricky Hunt*. Not sure how I can describe Ricky? Hyper comes to mind. Always rushing about, chasing his men, I was glad he wasn't my foreman. Our supervisor was a guy called *Ken Lawrence*. Now I still have contact with Ken, albeit only the occasional email although he has recently popped up as a Facebook friend. There was certainly no love lost between Ken and Jim Ferris, in fact, I can safely say Ken hated Ferris.

I had seen Ken around the plant occasionally, to be honest, I thought he was a clerk. He used to wear these largely flared trousers that must have been fashionable once, so once he became our foreman, he was referred to as "Baggy trousers."

Poor old Ken, he certainly went from the fat into the frying pan. Way too nice a guy to be a foreman. He used to be an avid stamp collector. Many a night shift I'd walk in the office and he'd have all these different stamps laid out on his desk.

Unfortunately for Ken, he was way to laid back. He didn't bollock any of us on his shift. He became known as "Easy Ken," on the other shifts. Something Jim Ferris soon picked up on. I'd given being a Shop Steward a rest for a while, Bill Cleary still held this grudge against me and I had other things going on in my life at that time. Now, I was friendly with a few of the security guards, and good job I was. They became our early warning system. Jim Ferris, for reasons I can't explain started coming in and checking up on us in the middle of the night. He wouldn't dare do it on the two other shifts, I know that Tony Lynch would have said to him, 'Well you're here now, I'm going home to my bed'. Jim Ferris had it in for Ken and hated our shift, so he would come in at 3 am and try and catch us asleep, *allegedly*. But luckily as Jim drove through the gate, one of the security guards would ring Ken, and he'd shoot around making sure we were hard at it. Many a time Ferris would check on me. I might have been a bit bleary-eyed, but I was working.

Only once did Ken let me down, and it caused a near riot. I am pretty placid these days, but back then it didn't take a lot for me to blow up. We used to work 37.5 hours weekly shifts, so each week I'd get my pay slip and if I hadn't done any weekend overtime, that's what I got paid for. We used to get our payslips on a Thursday. This particular day I strolled in and Ken handed it to me. I opened it and couldn't work out why it showed 37.25? I'd been docked 15 minutes. I stood there trying to work out if I'd been late the previous week. I knew I hadn't, I was never late. These were the days when we still clocked in and out. So, I questioned Ken.

'I'm fifteen minutes short here, Ken.'

'Oh .... Don't worry about it, I'll give you a no break.'

This meant he'd mark down that I'd worked through

my lunch break and would get 30 minutes overtime. To most people, they would have accepted this and let it go.
Not me.
'Why am I fifteen minutes short, Ken? I wasn't late last week, I didn't clock out early?'
Ken sat there all flustered, then the truth came out. The week before we were on the late shift. Jim Ferris had done one of his surprise visits. How sad, he wanted to come in and check up on us on a Friday evening. So about fifteen minutes before going home time I walked past Ken and Ferris and said goodnight. Went upstairs, washed up, came down and clocked out at 11 pm.
Now Ken let me down. Ferris told him to dock me fifteen minutes for going off in his eyes early. This is a Friday late shift when we had no production working. Ken being Ken, he didn't like confrontation, docked my time and didn't tell me. To say I lost it was an understatement. I can honestly say it was the only time I fell out with Ken, I felt really pissed off. Trying to hide it made it worse. Jim Ferris office was directly above, Usain Bolt wouldn't have got up those stairs quicker. I burst through the door and his clerk Maltese Joe said he was busy. Busy my arse, I went through without knocking and Ferris absolutely shit himself. I was so angry. Of course, he tried to justify it, but he knew if I took it further he was on a loser. I won't write down what was said, let's just say we had a heated debate that ended with him giving my time back. So, if our relationship was already fragile, it was the straw that broke the camel's back that day.

After that fracas, life for Ken became even more difficult. If there was a problem, Ferris would stick the blame on Ken and our shift. I can remember an incident with some white cellulose paint. Because our shift was weak, Jim Ferris gave us all the shit jobs. I came in on a late shift and Ken told me we had to paint the white on the Zebra crossing outside the plant.

'What, in the dark?' I enquired. It couldn't be done till all production had gone home, so after 6 pm. Ken was always reluctant to say no to Ferris. In the end, Ken agreed and said he would leave Ferris a note saying we couldn't paint in the dark.

'Let's at least get the paint out of the stores.' He suggested.

So, I went with him in our little electric buggy to the stores and got the last four cans of white cellulose paint that was in stock. Now I think we were cursed never to get this zebra crossing painted. As we drove back to the office, two cans flew off the buggy and the contents flew everywhere. The next few hours were spent mopping the mess up. Trust me when I tell you the paint fumes made you high. Anyway, I eventually cleaned it up best I could, I had to get some black spray paint and go over the area again. End of the matter as far as I was concerned.

Wrong.

Next afternoon I go to work and immediately I'm summoned to Ferris's office.

Ken was already there looking like a naughty schoolboy.

'Where's the paint, Whitehead?'

'Good afternoon to you, too.'
'Where's the paint?'
'What paint?'
'You drew four cans of white cellulose paint out yesterday, where are they?' I smelt a rat, and I looked at Ken.
'Tell him, Ken.'
'I've already said we had an accident and lost two cans.'
'Where're the other two cans, Whitehead?' Oh my god, I stood there and the penny dropped. I won't write what happened to the other two cans because to be honest I don't know. They had mysteriously disappeared? Let's just say the supervision in those days were allowed to park their cars behind the office. I won't point the finger!
I kept quiet and pleaded my innocence. In the end, I took Ferris's advice and I went off and multiplied. Let's say things between Ken and me were a bit fragile for a few days after that incident. Now I thought that was the end of the affair. But I should have known better, Ferris wouldn't let it go. One Friday morning he asks me to accompany him to a local builder's merchant. He buys a large can of white cellulose paint.
'They still haven't got any in the stores,' he informed me.
'Get that bloody zebra crossing painted tomorrow, I'm getting my arse chewed by the plant manager.' Now the zebra crossing was directly outside the main foyer.

'Block half and paint it, then block and paint the other half. Lock this paint in your locker until tomorrow.'
As far as I was concerned, I had an easy Saturday morning's overtime coming up …. Or so I thought.
Next morning, I get myself prepared. I sorted out the paint brushes, some masking tape and then loosened the lid off the paint tin then sat it back on it. Now the Central maintenance office and workshop were located at the back of the factory, so I had a bit of a walk carrying the full tin of paint.
Enter Roy English. Mr Toot, I used to call him. He was one of the wooden rubbish guys, he drove a small tractor and pulled all the rubbish bins from around various areas of the plant. We had big rubbish bins on wheels. So, Roy would collect and replace them. Now, these tow tractors had a small cab as they had to tow these bins outside to the back of the plant where they were emptied.
So, just as I started to make my way to the front of the factory he pulled up next to me.
'Where you going, Ginger?'
'Outside the foyer, I'm repainting the zebra crossing.'
'Jump in, I'll give you a lift.'
'Just be careful of the paint, I've loosened the lid.'
Roy took the tin of paint off me and sat it down between his legs, behind the gear levers. I climbed into the cab and tucked myself just to one side of him.
We start off, and we're having a general chit chat when he turned a sharp left by the engine assembly. You can guess what's coming. The whole tin tipped

over, the tin emptied all over his foot and went everywhere over the floor of the cab.
I didn't know whether to laugh or cry. I had Roy saying, 'I don't believe you, Ginger.' As he spoke his voice started to get higher as the fumes engulfed the cab.
'Stop for Christ sake,' I shouted.
Roy pulled up and I climbed out. I took the tin out and it had about half an inch left in the bottom. It was then that I saw the white paint dribbling out from under the tractor cab.
'Take the tractor outside,' I shouted to Roy.
He drove off and proceeded to leave a white line behind him as he went along.
I end up going and getting a couple of tins of black spray and black out the trail Roy had left behind. I eventually follow this white line outside to where Roy had parked up on a grass verge. He stood there, one leg looking like he had a white wellington boot on. High as a kite from the fumes, giggling and smoking a roll up. Again, he shouted, 'I don't believe you, Ginger.'
Anyway, I went and collected some rags and between us, we mopped up the paint in the cab. I then give it a coat of the black spray and it looked to me, okay.
Enter, Vehicle Repair fitter Ronnie Wood.
Dear old Ron, what a nice man he was, I say was because this story is going back at least thirty-five years. He'd be pushing ninety now. Having said that, so would Roy. I can't believe he'd still be alive, not after he'd got himself hooked on paint fumes.

Ron told Roy to bring the tractor to the Vehicle Repair shop.
'I have some stuff that will clean that all up.' Now bear in mind we're talking about a battered old tractor, anyway it was Roy's pride and joy, so off he went.
I continued my way back inside and checked I'd covered all the trail of paint. I got back to base and saw Roy and Ronnie with the said tractor. As I approached, I can see that Ron has cleaned all the paint off! The black paint, the cab was now back to showing all the white paint. I think that's the first time I used the word Muppet. In fact, a pair of muppets. I was more concerned about facing Jim Ferris on Monday. The zebra crossing still not done, I expected the worst. Just about my luck, I was on the early shift Monday. I clocked in and got changed. I walked into the office and straight away Ken informs me Ferris is wanting to see me. I looked at Ken, he had fear in his face.
'Calm down, Ken. I'm not facing a firing squad.'
'He's fuming, Trevor.'
'Fuck him, it was an accident.' Brave words from the condemned man.
So, I ambled upstairs, the clerk sat there, not Moody, he'd gone by then. Maltese Joe, he cheered me up no end.
Now Joe, as you may have guessed, originated from Malta. He had a Maltese accent and was a real doom and gloom merchant.
'He in da office waiting to see you, he, not a happy chappy. You gonna get your arse kicked.'

I made a mental note to do one of my speciality phone calls on him at a later date.
So, I walked in without knocking and there was Jim sitting behind his desk.
'What is it with you and this bloody zebra crossing? What the hell happened this time?'
So, I relay the story, exactly as it happened. As I got to the bit of finding Roy with his white leg, Jim burst out laughing. I mean really laughing. It started me off and I struggle to finish the story. It must have taken me ten minutes to get to the end as I kept stopping because I was laughing so much. Jim Ferris, I not lie, he was crying with laughter. Eventually, we both settled down.
'I have to say, I was going to bollock the life out of you. But that is the funniest thing I've ever heard in a long time. Go on, get to work.'
I don't know, as I write about this incident, I've sort of softened a bit about Jim Ferris. I guess outside of work he was a decent enough chap. Ken Lawrence wouldn't agree with me I know.
Jim disappeared soon after we got taken us over by another company. They started getting rid of a lot of the dead wood, so the General Foreman role ceased to exist. He got offered a normal foreman's role, but I think his pride got in the way and he retired at fifty-three. I heard through the grapevine he passed away last year. With Jim Ferris gone, Maltese Joe was shipped downstairs into the foreman's office. I bided my time and then an opportunity arose that I couldn't resist. Enter Colin Gittings, AKA, Elton.

Now Elton was a sludge king driver. He'd tow a large tank around and suck out all sorts of crap from machines, drains, all sorts. He had a cocky strut about him did our Elton, but one particular day I killed two birds with one stone. We were on the late shift and impatient Elton was trying to squeeze his tractor and tank through a small gap. A contractor had parked his Transit van in the way. Elton sat there for a minute tooting his horn. I was watching from above, I was up a ladder checking a hoist. Next thing I see Elton attempt to drive through the gap. Not a wise choice, he drove off leaving a long dent in the side of the van. About twenty minutes later I watched the contractor return. He climbed straight into the van and drove off. He'd not seen the dent along the side.

"You lucky bastard Elton," I thought.

Next afternoon I decided I could have some fun. So as soon as I was at work I used an internal phone and called the office. Joe answered.

'Central maintenance.' In my best-disguised voice, I spoke to Joe.

'Who's speaking?'

'It's Joe, the clerk.'

'Hello Joe, it's Fred from personnel.' There wasn't a Fred working there at this time, but Joe didn't have a clue.

'Hello Fred, what can I do for you?'

'You have a Colin Gittings working for you?'

'Yes, he is due at work shortly. He on da late shift.'

'Could you send him over to personnel as soon as he arrives.'

'Sure, what he do?'
'He's in a lot of trouble Joe, keep this to yourself, but he caused a lot of damage to a contractor's van last night. Caused hundreds of pounds worth of damage. Drove off and told the contractor to fuck off.'
'Jesus Christ. I'll send him over as soon as he gets here.' I hung up, walked around the corner and straight into the office. Joe was alone.
'You seen, Elton?'
'No, not yet. Why?'
'You ain't gonna believe this.' He then told me word for word the conversation we just had on the phone. Of course, I played along.
'I don't believe it.'
'Don't believe it? I've just had Fred from personnel on the phone.'
Timing it just right, enter Elton.
'You mister, you in big trouble. Don't get changed, go straight to Personnel, Fred is waiting for you.'
'Fred?'
'Don't act stupid. Fred, he personnel officer.'
Well, I've never seen the blood drain out of a person's face quicker than that day. The cockiness had gone as the realization of his previous night's exploits hit home.
'What you been up to, Elton?' I enquired.
'Nothing.'
'Nothing.' Shouted Joe.
In walked Ricky Hunt, early shift foreman about to go home.
'What's all the shouting about.'
'Ask him.' Joe points at Elton.

‘He been summoned to personnel, he crash into contractor’s van, caused hundreds of pounds of damage. Then drives off and tell the contractor to fuck off.’

‘No, I didn’t,’ pleaded Elton.

‘Come on, I’ll take you over in the buggy.’ Fair play to Ricky Hunt, he would always try and defend his men, even though Elton’s foreman was Ken Lawrence. I watched the pair drive off in the buggy. Mission accomplished.

I got myself changed, walked back to the office just in time to watch Joe have a hissy fit. Elton stood outside, back to his cocky self.

‘How’d you get on, Elton?’

‘It was a bloody wind-up. Ricky just had a go at Joe about it.’

I walked into the office as Joe slammed the phone on the floor. Ken had arrived by now and was standing with Ricky.

‘You finished now, Joe?’

‘These men, they taka the piss out of me.’

‘What’s happened?’ I ask.

‘Don’t ask,’ answered Ricky.

I walked out smiling.

I once saved Elton from a guaranteed pummelling. He came into work one morning like Mr Angry. He was a bit tubby, Elton. A bit like his namesake. He had the classic “Drop gut.” You know, the belly poking out from under your belt. Not like me who was just fat. So, not what you would describe as a highly tuned athlete.

'What's up with you?'
Turned out he had a bit of road rage at the traffic lights outside the factory the previous evening.
'I recognised the bloke, he works on engine machining.' Good luck with that I thought and left him to it. Heading over to the hoist crib where I was based I bumped into a guy named Brian Harris. Now Brian was always okay with me, I'd often stop for a chat and a laugh. Now, Brian had a fearsome reputation. He had a boxer's nose and you could tell he kept himself fit. Every now and again I'd hear a rumour about Brian's latest dust-up. The latest one I heard was where he stopped at some traffic lights and three guys stuck their fingers up at his wife. So, he got out of his car and knocked the three of them out. Now, I'm not saying it didn't happen, but the time a story about him reached me the exaggeration level would have risen a few notches. So, it was most probably one man. Always take things with a pinch of salt with stories like that. It's a bit like me when I told Barry Campagna I was in the original lineup of the Bay City Rollers. He believed that for about eighteen months until he realised they were all Scottish.
This particular morning, Brian's like a raging bull.
'Hey, Trevor. You got a guy who works over your side called Elton John?'
Well, it didn't take a rocket scientist to work out who Elton's road rage was with. So, I tried to reason with him.
'Yes, in fact, he's looking for you.'
'Send him over, I'll knock him into next week.' I could see the veins in Brian's head protruding.

'Listen, Brian. He told me he had a bit of road rage incident with you last night. He wants to come over and apologise, he's been having a few problems with the wife. You know how it is.'
'Well, we've all been there, Trev. Alright if he comes over and apologises that's the end of it.'
'Cheers Brian.' I then had to do an about turn and head back and track down Elton. Luckily, I caught up with him on his way over to hunt down Brian Harris.
'Alright, Elton?'
'I will be once I find this bloke.'
'Oh, I know who it is, it's a guy called Brian Harris. I've just spoken to him and he's very keen to meet you.'
'That name rings a bell.'
'Bell being the operative word here, Elton. That's what you'll be hearing once he chins you. For Christ sake man, go and apologise before he rips your head off.' I watched him walk off, the strut had definitely disappeared.

Another character I have fond memories of is John Levy. AKA Jolly Green.
Now John was a compulsive gossip and had an uncontrollable laugh.
Now when I say uncontrollable, I'm not joking.
One of our lads passed away, Ricky Redmond. Now Ricky was our overtime monitor. A job he took very seriously. Thursday mornings a sheet of paper would appear on the office window letting us know who was working the weekend. Ricky would study it and if there was a mistake he'd tear into the office to get it

corrected. At the time, he made it that if you weren't working the weekend, but managed to get overtime in another department, he'd still book you. We had a guy in our department named Geoff Lilley, AKA Catweazel. Now Geoff loved to go touring America. So, he would go off and find overtime anywhere he could. Ricky would find out and book him. This resulted over a period of time in Geoff being hundreds of hours in front of everybody else. Not a problem until a new guy would be transferred in. The rule being he would go on the overtime rota plus one hour below the bottom man. Poor sod would have to wait at least a year before he would get any overtime. Ricky wouldn't budge, our Shop Steward at the time was weak. It was nearing time for a comeback. Anyway, let's not run off to that period yet.

So poor old Ricky had a heart attack and passed away. He'd had heart trouble for a while, so not too much of a shock. We get time off to attend Ricky's funeral. I'm standing next to Jolly, luckily near the back of the church. Up stepped foreman Ricky Hunt to say a few words, all was going well until he mentioned that Ricky had been a good organiser. I whispered to Jolly. 'He certainly was on that overtime rota.' Well, big mistake. Jolly starts laughing, he starts a few of the others off. We then have to try and make it look like were crying. Unfortunately, by now, Jolly is down on his hands and knees. What a show he made of himself. I just hope Ricky was looking down and enjoying the show.

Having said that, I doubt it. He didn't take kindly to a little camera joke at his daughter's wedding.

He'd invited a few of us to the evening reception, about six of us attended. We and our wives were sat around a table. I'd noticed Ricky taking the odd photo. I blame the drink for what I did next. Ricky had hit the floor to dance with his daughter. While all that was going on, I walked past his table and whipped the camera into my pocket and head into the toilet. With the aid of a couple of others, we take photos of my arse and manhood. I walk back and slip the camera back on his table. Now you have to remember this is pre-digital age. This is the Kodak Instamatic, a roll of film age. Take the film to Boots the chemist and come back the following week to look at your twenty-four exposures. Exposure being the key word here. Now Ricky Redmond must have been on the shift before mine, because I can still picture him now, Standing, at the bottom of the stairs, hands on hips, roll up in his mouth, looking rather angry. Obviously waiting to speak to me, I tried to play it cool.

'Alright, Rick?'

'Alright ... You C***'

'Whoa, easy on the insults.' He pulled a photo out that showed my cock and balls.

'I knew it was you as soon as my daughter showed me. You're the only c*** I know with ginger pubes.'

Caught, bang to rights. The curse of the redhead. I think he was more upset because he'd given the film to his daughter to get developed. So, I guess it was a bit of a shock to her seen my arse and three-piece suite staring back at her.

Let's get back to Jolly, for some unknown reason, my dad had taken to Jolly. They remained friend's years after they had both retired. If ever he saw me he would always start the conversation by asking me, 'What's the news?' Followed by, 'How long so and so been dead?' He had this fascination with people's death. He looked like an undertaker so maybe that's why. Jolly used to have his morning tea break with dad. Every third week when I was on the early shift I'd join them. Many a time my dad would say something funny and we'd have Jolly rolling around the floor in hysterical laughter. Now Jolly, as gormless as he looked, had married well later life. His wife Val was a top personnel officer at a large bank. At the time, she earned three times what Jolly did. He had a nice house and both had new cars. It was the time the video recorder had just come out. The early ones, the ones with the piano keys and the wired remote would set you back around three hundred pounds. A lot of money back then, out of my price range at the time. But Jolly obviously could afford one and had great pleasure telling us about the wonders of this new gadget. There weren't many video stores around at the beginning. Within a couple of years, the market exploded and video stores became a huge success. A few of the lads and myself even ran our own mobile video store at work. I'll come to that story later in the book. Our mobile shop was named "The tug club." Might give you an idea of what taste we catered for.

Jolly told me that he'd got free membership to a video store in Chelmsford, where he bought the video player and where he lived. Time for a phone call. That evening, armed with the name of the shop where he'd bought the video player and the video shop, I called his number.
'Hello, who's speaking?'
'Good evening Mr Lovy, it's Sid from the video store.'
'Hang on, I need to turn the TV down.' Typical Jolly.
'Right, I can hear you now. Did you say you're calling from the video shop?'
'That's right Mr Lovy.'
'Levy, my name is Levy.'
'Oh, I'm sorry about that Mr Levy. Now, because you purchased your video player from such and such, you get free membership to our video store, ten free films with free delivery.'
'That's a great deal.' Jolly loved a bargain.
'What sort of films do you like?'
'Well, I like thrillers.'
'Don't we all, maybe I can send one of my colleague's round. He'll have a lot of films you can choose from. I have your address.'
'That would be great. How long can I keep the films for?'
'Maximum three nights, after that it's a pound a night.'
'That's fair.'
'Can I ask Mr Levy; would you like my colleague to bring round some porn?'

'Err ...... Can your colleague come around tomorrow evening, but before seven? My wife comes home around seven thirty.'
'No problem, Mr Levy.'

Next morning at tea break, Jolly tells my dad and me all about the video offer, even about the porn. He walked off and my dad said to me what a good deal Jolly had got.
'I doubt it, dad. That was me who phoned him.' It didn't end there. Next morning Jolly told us this video guy hadn't turned up.
'I'm going into that video shop on my way home this afternoon, ask them what their game is?'
Next morning my dad asked Jolly how he'd got on?'
'Denied making the phone call. I told them to stuff their membership.'

It was amazing how gullible Jolly was. A few months later he told my dad and I the saga of his new 32" TV. He'd ordered it at an HMV store in Chelmsford. He'd waited in the previous evening and it never arrived.
'Val's going to ring them this morning.' Now the mighty Valerie according to Jolly was not a woman to mess with. Later in the day, I could see Jolly had the hump.
'What's up with you?' He then tells me he'd phoned Val and basically after what I could imagine was a one-way phone call, Valerie had told whoever to stuff their TV.
'I had my heart set on that TV, Sony 32". Time for another phone call.

I waited until six, I knew Jolly usually made it home by five-thirty.
'Mr Levy?'
'Yes, who's speaking?'
'Dave Smithers, customer services for HMV.'
'You've got a nerve ringing me after the way you spoke to my wife this morning.'
'That's why I'm ringing, Mr Levy. The assistant your wife spoke to has been fired. We at HMV pride ourselves on our customer service.'
'What service, we sat in last night waiting for the new TV to come. It didn't, and when my wife phoned the store all she got was an answer phone!'
'Deep apologies Mr Levy. This really isn't good enough.'
'Too true it's not.'
'How far from the Chelmsford store do you live, Mr Levey?'
'About ten minutes.'
'Do you drive, Mr Levy?'
'Yes.'
'Okay, I have a slight problem you see. All the drivers are out on deliveries. If you can get to the store before seven, I'll make sure your Sony 32" TV is there waiting for you. I'll instruct the shop to give you a two-hundred-pound discount.'
'I'm on my way.' Jolly hung up.
Now I knew the discount would be enough to reel him in. What with Jolly's surname and nose, he had to be Jewish. I can remember when Nescafe coffee was doing a promotion for something or another. Jolly started collecting the coffee labels. One

morning I was driving to work when I passed the big recycling bins. You know the type, different colours for different things. One for plastic, one for cardboard, one for bottles. Anyway, as I drove past I noticed Jolly's car. I pulled up and as I looked I could see Jolly's feet poking out from the glass bin. He wriggled back out with a triumphant look on his face. He had an empty jar of Nescafe in each hand. If he saw a newspaper in a bin, he'd scour it for any money off vouchers. You can imagine being stuck behind him in a supermarket check-out.

Next morning, I once again never mentioned anything to my dad. Jolly turned up for the morning tea break fuming.

'You won't believe this George.' Jolly went all through the phone call part. I sat and kept my eyes on the newspaper, but my ears pricked.

'Sounds like they offered you a real bargain, John.' My dad was oblivious to the involvement of me.

'Bargain George? Do you know I drove straight to the shop, and guess what? You won't believe it, George. The bloody shop was shut, they close for half day on a Wednesday.'

How I kept a straight face I'll never know.

'Val is going to roast the customer services this morning. I wrote the guy's name down, Dave Smithers.'

'That's a small world, our window cleaner is called Dave Smithers.' Dad looked at me and the penny dropped.

My finest hour with Jolly was the new car hoax. Each month our company would do a raffle. Very good prizes at the time. We were a part of a big combine in the UK and the raffle was open to all plants. I can't remember the exact prizes but the top three were normally a new car, followed by large holiday vouchers right down to fifty pounds. I'm sure there were at least thirty prizes each month. Occasionally someone at our Plant would be lucky. I decided it was about time Jolly had a bit of luck. I was on the night shift so waited until Ken went off somewhere and snuck in and took some company headed writing paper and a company stamped envelope. I headed into an empty office and typed a letter informing Jolly he had won the top prize and there would be a presentation of the keys two days later outside the office. I also added that a photographer would be present from the company newspaper. I read it back and was happy with the finished article. I squiggled a signature and typed the name of the guy who always featured on the sheet of paper that came out monthly with the raffle results. I typed Jolly's name, his ID number and Central Maintenance on the envelope and slipped it into the internal post mail. I went home the next morning happy with life. In a way, I was sad not to see the fruits of my work, but in another way, I think I was better off being on nights as this letter to Jolly had worked better than expected. I'm a firm believer that the fewer people that know about your involvement in a wind-up, the better. So, I never mentioned anything to my dad, even though he rang me the next evening.

'Heard about Jolly?'
'No.'
'He's only won the top prize in the raffle, a bloody new Escort.'
'Lucky bastard, well they say money goes to money.'
'Big presentation outside the office at ten 'o' clock tomorrow morning.'
'Pity I'm on nights, I would have liked to see that.'
'I'll let you know how it goes.'
So that night I go to work and the news on Jolly's win is a hot topic. I try and play it cool as I'm beginning to worry things have got slightly out of hand. A phone call from my dad the next evening confirmed my fears.
'Was that you?'
'What?'
'Did you type that letter.' I couldn't lie to my dad.
'Yes, how'd it go?'
'Great. Jolly turned up in his best suit. Maltese Joe turned up in a suit too. Tony Lynch went and had a haircut and about fifty people were standing outside the office at ten. About ten minutes went by and people were getting restless. Tony instructed Joe to ring up and find out where the raffle people and photographer were. Five minutes later he comes out of the office shouting.
"They don't know nothing about it, the raffle not been drawn for this month yet." Everybody booed. The letter is now over in personnel. Don't worry, they haven't a clue who typed it.' Luckily for me, they didn't want to fingerprint everybody. The time I was back on the early shift it had all been forgotten.

I went to see Jolly a couple of years after he retired. He'd moved to Devon and I was on holiday for a week in the area. I went to see him and he looked well and still collecting the money off vouchers.
If you're still alive and read this John, sorry mate, but you were good entertainment.

Another guy I tormented around that time was an oiler named Bill McKay. Tall, grey-haired man, mild-mannered until you wound him up. I had him chase me around the factory one late shift.
I can't remember where I got this false rubber cock from. But I had some fun with it. It was impressive and a good nine inches long. It looked the real deal. You could fill it with water and if you squeezed it, it was like a water pistol. So now and again I'd fill it up, follow someone into the toilet and when they were mid-stream, I'd whip it out and start to pretend to relieve myself. Then turn to the guy and say hi while squeezing some water down their leg. Of course, before they got angry I'd whip it out and show them the joke penis. I must have been feeling a bit mischievous with Bill because I followed him in. Proceeded to do a pretend piss, then turned and really gave it a squeeze. It came out with such a force that it not only hit his leg and arm, the spray hit his face and glasses.
'Yer dirty bastard,' he shouted in his broad Scottish tone.
For some reason, I decided to leg it. I can honestly say, Bill McKay wanted to kill me. He chased me from

one end of the factory to the other. I was only in my late twenties and he was pushing sixty. But he wasn't going to give up. I don't think me giggling as I ran helped his mood. In the end, I surrendered. I stopped and held the rubber penis in the air. Poor Bill, he was knackered. But he just sat down and started laughing. Luckily for me, he'd seen the funny side of it. I had some laughs with that toy until it split, and I ended up with a crutch full of water.

I hit my thirties and a horrible thing happened at work. One of the tinsmiths dropped dead right in front of my dad and me. Wally Clarke had joined the tinsmiths late in life. There had been three tinsmiths since the plant opened, all around the same age. One of them, Ernie Hughes went to school with my dad, so they'd known each other a very long time. The other tinsmith was Bob Kent. Then came Larry Minchin, maybe ten years younger than the other three. They were all very good at their trade. At the time, they had more work than they could cope with, so they had Kevin Gill, a seventeen-year-old apprentice start with them. Nice lad and a very good footballer. But he was just into his second year of his apprenticeship. So, the company in their wisdom advertised on the notice boards for anyone with the sheet metal skills. Wally Clarke joined the team. He fitted in well and enjoyed the banter that came his way. You see, although Wally was the new "boy," he was about seven years older than my dad. But he kept himself busy and you could tell he enjoyed the work. He'd been working in the hydraulics for years, so I guess it

was nice to get away from the production side of things.
One morning I went and joined my dad for a tea break. Wally sat by his workbench maybe six feet away.
My dad told me that Wally hadn't been feeling well and had been to the medical for "indigestion."
We sat there reading our newspapers when Wally suddenly groaned and started to slide off his chair.
We rushed over to help him but he couldn't be saved.
None of us had a clue what to do. Time a first aider and the medical arrived Wally was dead. It was awful, I'd never seen a man die before and it shook me to my bones. Took me a long time to come to terms with that morning. It made me worry about my dad. Wally was only sixty, dad must have been around the fifty-three at the time.
I pestered the life out of him to get out. There were opportunities for him to get an early retirement. But he hung on for a while. Then one day he phoned me and said he was retiring on Friday. I was half relieved, but the other half of me knew I'd miss him terribly. I wouldn't say we were close, but he'd always been at the plant all the time I'd been there. He had remarried, mum and he had divorced some years earlier. Not the normal sort of setup, my dad married the woman and my mum married the husband. I won't go into all the gory details, but they did a bit of wife swapping and it went too far. My mum and her husband Peter moved to Manchester for a while before returning to Essex. When Dad retired he told me he was selling up and moving to Norfolk. So, I

was a bit surprised when he phoned me and said he'd bought a new bungalow in a place called Burton upon Stather.
'Where's that?' I ask.
'North Lincolnshire.' So, I go out to my car and look this place up on my roadmap. Basically, he was moving to Scunthorpe, or to village six miles further on. He liked it up there, I hated the place. Cold and gloomy, and that was in July.
I never got on with his wife and over time my visits became less and less. We'd talk on the phone weekly, but that was about it. He was just coming up to eighty when he passed away.

The other tinsmiths all disappeared in time. Engine machining was on the way out. Bob and Ernie left within a year of my dad. Kevin stuck it out for a while but left in his late twenties. Larry retired at fifty-five and became a postman. I bumped into him a few years later in Cardiff of all places. I'd gone to Wales to watch Southend United in a minor trophy final. LDV vans I think. We'd made it to the final along with Blackpool. It was billed as the battle of the Seasiders. It was played at the Millennium stadium because they were in the throes of building the new Wembley Stadium. I was staying in the same hotel as Larry. He was down with his family and I hardly recognised him. He had lost loads of weight and looked really good. He told me he was into fitness and with the amount of walking he was doing delivering mail, he was in the best shape he'd been for years. So, it came as a shock when I heard he had dropped dead in a gym.

Turned out he had a massive heart attack while on a rowing machine. Such a shame, he was a lovely guy Larry. His daughter was expecting her first child when he passed away, tragic.

I think when you work at a place with a huge workforce, news of a death was inevitable. You'd hear of someone passing away quite often. Now, this is meant to be a fun read, so let's not hang around on this subject for too long. Death is death, inevitable for all of us, we just don't want to be reminded of it. Cue a little story of when I became a pension trustee with Mr Happy, AKA Paul Norris. We were asked to make a small contribution and introduce ourselves in the yearly pension magazine. I can't remember what I wrote, most probably the importance of being in a well-run company pension scheme. I never knew what Paul wrote until the magazine arrived through the post. He made such a great opening statement, it's up there with the "Could have been worse, he could have broken a leg, gaff."

I opened the page and there was a photo of Paul. I'm sure he won't mind me saying, but he has the face for a radio presenter, so not exactly photogenic. If I thought that was bad, I wasn't prepared for his opening statement emblazoned underneath the horror photo. In big letters, it read:

"We're all going to get old and die."

I suppose in his defence it could be argued that he didn't beat about the bush. I can't be too harsh with Paul. He studied hard for a degree and went on to better things. Good on you mate. But let's not get ahead of ourselves here, let's get back to the eighties.

Chapter 3

Time for a comeback

The eighties turned out to be a funny decade for me. For some reason, I became a bit accident prone. I don't know why, but one particular late shift Ricky Hunt was my foreman.
Wrong place wrong time, he spotted me just as I was about to go for my lunch break. That would be 7 pm. 'Trevor, do me a favour. Could you drive this tractor and park it up outside the gardener's hut?'
Cursing under my breath I jumped aboard and drove this old tractor outside and up the hill to where the gardener's hut was situated. Now I'd always fancied being one of the gardeners, in the summer they would be cutting grass or doing the verges, shirt off. Much better than being inside the factory. Now, being I was late for my lunch break I thought I would be clever. Instead of walking back to the main building on the road, I decided to take a shortcut and run down the steep grass bank. I never knew what idiot left the manhole cover off, but I managed to find it and suddenly I had dropped down and was saved only by my arms sticking out. I can remember the shock, followed by the pain as I heaved myself out. Sitting there I felt I was lucky not to have fallen right down, I might still be there now. I could see it in the papers, "The mystery of the missing tractor plant worker. Clocked in and was never seen again." The pain from my legs started and I pulled my trouser leg

up and could see I had ripped all the skin off my shins, both legs.
'Bollocks,' I shouted. There was no one about, so I had to hobble back to the office. Ricky was sitting behind his desk, feet up and eating a sandwich.
'All done?'
'I've had an accident.'
'What happened?' So, I relay the story and he starts to laugh.
'Teach you to take a shortcut. Go and have your lunch break.'
'What about these?' I dropped my trousers and the bottom of my legs were now a bloody mess.
'Jesus Christ, Trevor.' We never had medical coverage on a late shift, just first aiders. I can't remember who our first aider was at that time, but I can remember him telling Ricky I should go to casualty. So off we go and after the usual long wait I get seen and patched up. Ricky dropped me in the car park next to my car.
'Go home and rest, I'll pay you till eleven.' He drove off and I climbed into my car. I looked at my watch, it was 10.40pm. You were all heart, Ricky.

Now a funny thing happened after that. The next morning, I woke up, I was feeling bit groggy, my legs were sore and I was busting for a pee. So, I limped to the bathroom and while I'm relieving myself I glanced at the mirror. Looking back at me was a Red Indian? I check myself and I'm covered in a rash from head to toe. Panicking I phone the doctors. Well as we know, the doctor's receptionists are a breed amongst themselves. It doesn't matter what you say, you can't seem to get past them and speak to an actual doctor. To cut a long story short after about ten minutes of a thorough grilling, she agreed to send a doctor round to see me after the surgery had closed. By Early afternoon he arrived, took one look at me and told me I had measles? I was twenty-five at the time. I had a bad couple of weeks, what with the symptoms that come with adult measles, and my legs were very tender. I was living on my own at that time, so good old mum came over and spent a few days nursing her Chocolate Soldier.

Back at work and things were changing on the union front. The self-proclaimed union governor, Convenor Bill Cleary had left the company. The potbellied, goatee-bearded, pipe smoking, trilby hatted dwarf had gone. Praise the Lord. At the time, it had been three or four years since I was last a shop steward. I can't remember who our shop steward was at the time, but an unlikely person contacted me to consider standing at the forthcoming shop steward elections. Enter the *rat*. Now I won't say too much about Mr *Rat* at this point in the book. He will feature heavily as we move along. But, fair play to the *rat*, he encouraged me to stand. I did, and I walked it. I'm not sure why I always did well in elections? I would say it was my great personality, charisma, and the way I fought for my men. In reality, it is most probably whoever faced me in the elections were more unliked than me. So, I was back, the brash and cocky Trevor had returned. Jim Ferris was still

General Foreman at that time, he hated the fact I was again the shop steward. He had to tread a tad more careful with me, after all, I had the clout of the mighty union behind me.
George Catton was now the convenor. Old school, he was the deputy under Cleary, so the natural successor. I found a lovely short news clip on YouTube, of the Plant in 1984. There's a brief interview with George Catton in the report. Certainly, worth a watch and you can see a bit of the eighties style of vehicles we were building at the time.
I didn't know much about George until I came back from the wilderness. He was one-half of the double act, George and George. I likened them to the Two Ronnie's, or Morecambe and Wise.
The other George I knew well. George Sharpe. As I sit here and write this I can visualise his face. He reminded me of the late American comic who played "Bilko." Phil Silvers. He may have had a resemblance to Phil, but he had the voice of the Carry-On actor, the late Bernard Bresslaw. I liked George immensely, he was glad I had come back into the shop steward's fold. He could tell the most entertaining stories, none I care to repeat in this book. He was a great supporter of George Catton and it was rare to see one of them without the other. One thing George Sharpe struggled with was staying awake. I can recall being sent to Boreham House for some seminar with a few other stewards, George being one of them. The Manager running this seminar was Michael Law. He was a bit of an "Oh look at me, aren't I wonderful" type of person in my opinion. Obviously well thought

of by the company as he was sent to Brazil for a number of years. Unfortunately, they sent him back. I was sitting the other side of the room to George and as I watched I knew it wouldn't be long before his head would start rocking and the eyes rolling. The problem George had, he wasn't discreet about it. He'd eventually get his head comfortable and within minutes he would start to snore. My god, I don't know how many times Michael Law banged the table that day. He wasn't amused. In defence of George, we all struggled with Michael Law's presentation. Not sure if Michael is still with us, he must be nearing eighty if he is. If you read this Michael, sorry, but you were boring and monotonous.

It must have been around this time that the inter-departmental cricket league started. I was a decent player at school but not picked a ball up since. A notice went up about the formation of this league and an opportunity to register your team. A few of us in Central Maintenance fancied this, so we entered our department. The crux of the team was, Bob Fagg, Bob Fellows, Brian Crease and myself. All we needed now was another seven players. We managed to secure a foreman by the name of Harry Geering, he was a supervisor in the tool room. My fellow hoist-man Steve Battle stepped forward. I have some lovely stories about Steve later in the book. He was pigeon-toed but had a good eye for the ball. Arthur Rixon said he would play. A skilful electrician and Tottenham Hotspur supporter. Over fifty, but could still bowl a decent delivery. It was a wise move signing up Arthur. His wife Mary would come along to support us, armed with a tin of homemade cakes. We recruited a guy called Gordon Beattie as our wicket keeper. I'm sure Gordon won't mind me mentioning his stout figure. Ideal wicket keeper build, we thought at the time. He failed to mention that his nickname was "Teflon." With the allowance of two guest players, we just about scraped a team together for our first match. Our last player was a guy called Steve Holman. More suited to playing darts, he could walk, so he was in. I must admit when I watched him run his pace was deceptive ... He was a lot slower than he looked. The games were played at the company club in the evenings. Equipment was supplied and we turned up a tad apprehensive.

Our first game was against a team from the offices, an unknown entity, but they looked impressive as they warmed up, a few of them were in cricket whites, so I didn't hold out a lot of expectation. The format was twenty overs a team, each player except the wicketkeeper would bowl two overs. If you hit 25, you'd retire but could come out and bat again if everybody else was out. Although we looked a motley crew, we gave it our best shot. Because we hadn't played before we didn't know who was capable of what. Arthur turned up in his whites. The only one of us that had actually played cricket for a club. Bob Fagg was captain. Bob was a bigger version of the late 1966 World Cup winner Alan Ball. Same golden hair and the high-pitched voice.

Unfortunately for Bob his voice never broke. He wore glasses those days. Years later he decided to have his

eyes lasered. There's a funny story of him about to drive a tractor out of the factory when someone shouted at him.
'Mind the axle stand.'
'Don't you worry about that, I have 20 – 20 vision.' He called back. He then proceeded to drive straight over the axle stand!
I did try to contact Bob while researching this book but never heard anything back. He must also be pushing eighty now, so I'm guessing social media and emails are foreign to him? Right, back to the cricket. Bob thought it would be a good idea to get Arthur to open the batting. Now Arthur was a bit like the Cockney comedian Tommy Trinder. He'd pout his lips and say, "Alright you lucky lads, let's be having you." Bandy-legs, he would never have made it as a goalkeeper. Now it's funny how some things stick in your mind. I can remember this match as if it was yesterday.
We lost the toss and were put into bat first. Bob Fagg decided to open the batting with Arthur. We sat at the boundary watching the game unfold and eating Mary's cakes. It soon became apparent that Arthur was pitched in for a five-day test match. He obviously had designs on being the Central Maintenance's "Geoffrey Boycott." Unfortunately, we only had twenty overs. Arthur blocked the first five, then hit a single off the last ball. So, he had run to the other end to face the next over. The words déjà vu crossed my mind as Arthur adopted the blocking technique for the second over. After two overs, we were 2 for 0. At this rate, we would be setting our opposition

the mighty total of twenty-one to win the match. Over number three and at last Bob Fagg got the scoreboard moving. He had a good over, hit a couple of boundaries then ran Arthur out. Something Arthur would never forget. Of course, when he marched off after Bob had given him no chance of getting to the other end, we were full of sympathy for him.
'Did you see that? I was just getting my eye in.'
'Yes, Arthur. Terrible call by Bob.' Bob Fellows went out and joined Bob and we were getting some decent runs on the board. I can't remember everyone's individual scores, but the two Bob's, Brian Crease and myself all had a swing. The last few batsmen added a few more runs and I think we ended up with around a hundred runs. We were happy that we'd posted a score that wasn't too embarrassing.

(Funny, I have found an old photo of some of our team holding a cricket Trophy. The photo was taken behind the factory. We're not all in it, but the two Bob's, Arthur, Brian, Harry, Gordon and I are standing to attention. I have some type of shell suit top, skinny jeans and brown shoes. Deidre Barlow glasses and swept back hair. I look a right cock.)

Back to the game:

A bit like our batting, we didn't know who our better bowlers were. I knew I could bowl a fast ball, Bob Fagg could bowl a sort of mix between a spin and middle pace ball. Arthur said he could bowl and after lashing Bob about running him out, to appease him,

Bob said he could open the bowling. I had a chat with Bob and suggested he hold himself and me back for a few overs, try and use some of the others first. I didn't think it would be good to use up all our better bowlers at the beginning. So, we adopted the tactic of putting a better bowler on with a lesser bowler. To start with, it seemed to work. Hats off to Arthur Rixon. He had obviously lost a bit of pace, but he was accurate. He'd say he was fast to medium, I'd say he was medium to slow. But in his two overs, he skittled a couple of their players out and didn't give away many runs. Brian Crease could bowl a decent ball, Steve Battle, as expected had a good eye and bowled well. Bob Fellows who said he wasn't much of a bowler surprised himself and us by not giving much away and taking at least one wicket. We had them a rattled a bit, their run rate was creeping up. At the time, they were around 40 for 5. We'd got through twelve overs, so we were certainly in with a shout. Bob knew he still had me and himself to bowl. He decided to hold us back for the final push. Enter Steve Holman, and the wheels started to come off. If I thought Steve was a slow runner, nothing prepared me for the dolly's he was bowling. His first over gave away about thirty runs. I'm pretty certain all his six balls were boundaries, either a six or a four. The opposition was suddenly back in the driving seat. Bob threw me the ball. I walked down the other end to bowl. I then went about another ten feet down. The batsman must have wondered where the hell I was going, along with my team mates. One thing about me, I hate to lose. I ran into bowl like a demon

possessed, I thumped the ball down with such ferocity it cleared poor old Gordon Beattie's head by about ten feet. My attempted bouncer had given away four runs. Gordon walked up to me.
'Calm down big fella.' He handed me the ball as and as I walked back to bowl the batsman smirked. 'Same again mate.'
'I guess as I ran in he expected another fast delivery, I think he was already swinging as I let go of the ball. The ball came down the wicket and passed the batsman at half the speed of my previous ball. The batsman had swung the bat far too early. Out you go. I think I skittled a couple out that over. Bob couldn't risk another Steve Holman over at that stage so bowled himself. He bowled well and took a wicket, I bowled my second over and took another scalp. The time it came to Bob to bowl his second over the match was on a knife-edge. We had somehow managed to remove nine of them. The last two batsmen were at the wicket. They had plenty of overs in hand. Bob had one over left to bowl, Steve Holman had one to bowl and someone else who I can't remember had two to bowl. They only needed ten runs to win. After two or three balls, they'd reduced that target to six. The next moment will stay with me the rest of my life. Bob ran down to bowl, I think the man facing wanted to end the match in glory. He swung the bat and the ball flew up high and long towards the boundary. The ten of us watched as the ball went sky high and towards Steve Holman. He of the slow running technique. Arms pumping, he ran towards the fast dropping ball. Ten voices shouting

out to him, “Catch it.” After a little fumble that had ten hearts jumping, he held onto it.
My god, we had won.
What a night, you’d have thought we’d won the world cup the way we celebrated in the clubhouse after. None of us wanted to go home as we relived the game ball by ball. This motley crew had somehow managed to win a game. One of my fondest memories.

Of course, we soon came down with a bang in our next match where we got absolutely hammered. To be honest I’m not sure if we even won another game that season. It didn’t matter, we had our glory night and we dined on that for years. Happy days.

I had settled back into my shop steward’s role, I think I was always destined to be some form of representative. I loved to hammer my point of view across and take up any cases of wrongdoing. The first thing I did when I was elected was to stick to my campaign promise and scrap the current over time rota and introduce a fairer system. I wasn’t happy with this booking people’s hours if they found over time in another department. I also got rid of booking hours and just changed it to a simple rotation system. I gave the new layout to the three foremen and popped upstairs and gave one to Jimmy Ferris. For once he had something good to say.
‘Thank god for this. That was a terrible system you had before. Have you given Ricky a copy?’
‘I’ve given one to all three foremen.’

'Not Ricky Hunt, Ricky Redmond. He's the overtime monitor.'

I'd forgotten all about him.

'Not anymore, I'm taking that role, His days of "Book em Danno," have gone.'

'Good luck with that.'

I left Ferris's office and knew I was going to have a little battle on my hands. Ricky Redmond had been the overtime monitor since the year dot. He played merry hell when I told him. Went to see Ferris, who played the "Nothing to do with me," card. He went to personnel and eventually I was summoned over to see one of them.

I think this is a good point to mention the Personnel Department. I will be brief.

Ninety percent of them I didn't like. Especially later in my time at work. Once they started bringing in these graduates with absolutely no life skills, I didn't have time for any of them. I liked and respected the likes of Carl Curbishley, Dennis Morley and Ken Pocklington. Old school and world-wise. I can't remember who I dealt with, but I agreed to hold a ballot for the overtime monitor position. Honestly, I had serious issues to address and I was being sidetracked by Mr Angry. He was still smarting over the photos of my arse, cock and balls.

So, I stuck a notice up and I was expecting a two-horse race with Ricky Redmond. Elton tried to muddy the water by sticking his name in the hat. After a few choice words with him, he withdrew. In the end, Ricky received only two votes. He'd made a lot of enemies over the years.

Once I had dealt with Ricky, life as a shop steward became easier. George Catton was doing a good job as far as I was concerned. People like the *rat,* Alan Phillips and Geoffrey Martin Smith were all junior stewards.

I didn't realize it at the time, but those three would become key figures in the union, I grew old with these guys. Stewards came and stewards went. Some didn't last long. They wanted to become a shop steward for their own gain. Normally a grudge against a supervisor. Some were voted out by their membership. Any weakness was soon put to the test. Shop Steward elections were always a tense time for a shop steward. We had an election every biennial. The notice would go up on the boards and if you wanted to stand you had to go and see the convenor and get a nomination form. Now depending on who the guy was and what current steward he was wanting to replace, one of two things would happen. If it was a steward well-liked by the convenor, he would really try and put the prospective candidate off. I know this because I heard it first hand when the *rat* was the convenor.

'You sure you want to commit to this role for the next two years?'

'Well, I wouldn't be asking for a form if I didn't. That **** **** is beyond useless.'

'Really? And you think you can do better?'

'Well, I can try?'

'Trying's no good mate, you go away and really think about what you're doing.' Nine times out of ten the guy was never seen in the convenors office again.

If the convenor didn't like the steward, a completely different approach came about.
'Come in mate, you want a cup of tea?'
'That would be nice, cheers.'
'Trevor, make ****** a cup of tea will you.'
'So, you want to become a steward?'
'Well, I'd like to give it a shot.'
'You're just the type of steward we're looking for. Here, take a nomination form, get two signatures and bring it back to me before Friday. So how you been?'

Of course, later on, the said Steward who was now facing an election had heard the news and come in to see the convenor.
'Has that bastard ****** come in for a nomination form?'
'Yes, he has, but don't worry. I can't see him standing. I gave him a good talking to. Told him the pitfalls of being a steward. I'll be very surprised if he takes it any further.'

Back to George Catton.
I'd not heard any grumblings about George. He was a long-standing steward who had served under Bill Cleary for many years. To me he was a breath of fresh air after my time, I should add, short time under Bill Cleary.

I liked him. He had a dry sense of humour and a sharp brain. I can only liken to what happened to George, by using the way Tony Blair took over leadership of the Labour Party. I was going to say that he took over from Neil Kinnock. But that's not factually true. For a brief time, we had John Smith (until he keeled over in the shower) then Margaret Beckett for two months before Tony Blair was elected.

Now, Neil Kinnock was a good opposition leader but wasn't well liked by some of the MP's. Being Welsh obviously didn't help. But I've met Neil Kinnock. He is a very nice man and very sharp. But Tony Blair was ambitious and soon started a campaign that would belittle Neil and lead him to the leadership.

George Catton was a very nice man, as I've already stated he had a sharp brain. But his downfall was he wasn't a great public speaker. At least not in the eyes of some of the more prominent stewards that I have already mentioned. They were out to get him. The *rat's* ambitions couldn't wait any longer. A plan was hatched and I'm guessing each of those three was targeted to get support. The *rat* was making his bid to be the new convenor. Geoffrey Martin Smith had me in his sights.

He came to see me and told me the plan. I wasn't overjoyed about it in the beginning. My point of view was to let George see the remainder of his term out. I honestly can't remember how long he had left, I'm sure it was less than a year. But the prince in waiting was growing ever more impatient. Rumours started to leak out about George's inadequacies. With the

promise of a more active role in the committee swung it for me. I was ambitious and I knew that if I went against the *rat* in the vote and he got elected, then I'd be back in the Bill Cleary type scenario of having a pissed off convenor against me.
The meeting and vote of no confidence were awful to be involved with and witnessed. I had done it myself years previously with Bobby Graham. I wasn't overjoyed about doing it, but Bobby wasn't Steward material.
George Catton was. He'd been an engine machining steward for a number of years and knew his stuff. Being a convenor is a full-time role. You're transferred out of your department and I guess you come under the personnel department. So, George was voted out. The *rat* was voted in. Alan Phillips became the deputy. In a bid to curb George Sharp's anger he was elected as the plant Health and Safety Rep. Truth be told, I don't think George Sharpe ever forgave the *rat* for shoving his mate out.

George Catton didn't want to go back in the plant. You can't blame him. He'd worked his way up in the union to the pinnacle. Going back to being an operator in engine machining area wasn't a move he relished. Remember, he wasn't even a shop steward now. Personnel put him in a photocopying office for a while until they could work out what to do with him. In the end to save everyone's blushes he took early retirement. He cut a forlorn figure and you couldn't help but feel sorry for him. I will say this. At least he walked out with his head held high. Not like a dirty rat caught stealing the cheese. That moment was yet to come.

Chapter 4

Onwards and upwards.

By the mid nineteen eighties, things were settling down after the *rat's* successful coup. As promised I received my first responsibility within the union. I was now the canteen representative. Couldn't have happened to a more deserving steward than me. After all, I was a professional eater.

It was while I held this position that I had the taste of my first junket. Times were changing in the canteen. The lack of customers put the late shift service at risk. Paying two women to come in and serve maybe a maximum twenty dinners was never going to last. The *rat* was approached and I was sent with two other stewards to Bristol to look at the freeze dry food machines. We accompanied two managers from the canteen company and Ken Pocklington from Personnel who was also our driver. We were put up at a nice hotel in Bristol. Now the two stewards who came with me were Barry Mansfield the paint steward and Bill Hammond from the Product Engineering side.

We were left to our own devices the first night. For some reason, we met up in Bill's room and proceeded to empty his fridge. I can't remember much more about that night apart from a half recollection that we ended up in an Indian restaurant. We had breakfast the following morning in the hotel and then told to check out as we were travelling to a nearby factory to see these freeze-dried food machines in action. We had left the champagne unopened in Bill's room. It was twenty-five pounds for half a bottle. But the three of us decided to take the bottles. We checked out and got in the minibus. We had all said no when they asked if we'd touched the mini bar. Everyone else climbed in and as we started to drive off, looking across we could see the manager from the hotel running out.

'Keep driving', pleaded Bill who had gone into panic mode.

Ken, who was driving the minibus, pulled up and gave Bill a funny look.

'What's up with you?'

'Err ... Nothing. I just want to get there, I'm hungry.'

'You've just had your breakfast?' Bill tried to make himself smaller by sliding down his seat.

Ken wound his window down and the manager of the hotel gave him an envelope. I could hear Ken thanking the manager. The manager walked off and three of the men in the back sighed with relief.

Turned out the manager had given us a discount voucher each for that particular chain of hotel. That little incident with Bill I reminded him of for years.

We ended up at this small factory where they made the machines for the freeze-dried food. After plenty of samples, we headed home.

Although not ideal, it was better than nothing. I always remembered my first shop stewards meeting and poor Roy. So, I put the findings to the shop stewards committee and the freeze-dried food machines were soon prominent in the canteen.

There's a sad note to this story.

Barry Mansfield who was three or four years younger than me passed away a few years ago. He'd left work after the paint floor came downstairs and became more automated. He was a big guy, a very popular steward. I only saw him once after he left the plant. He stood in front of me in a garage when I was queuing to pay for some petrol. To be honest I didn't realise it was him until he turned around. He was now a taxi driver and had piled a lot of weight on. He was only around fifty when he passed away.

It was around this time that I had to take on another responsibility, this time work-wise. They wanted me to be a backup Grinding Wheel man. Just to cover holidays and sickness. Always one to add another string to my bow, I accepted the challenge. Now you may think that's a strange use of terminology, but I found it a challenge because the man who was going to train me was a notorious bullshitter. Although he has been dead a number of years, I'll save his family any embarrassment and call him "Billy."

Now Billy as a bloke was a decent enough fellow, or so I thought. A good union supporter and a skilful Grinding wheel man.

Unfortunately, he had a problem, he would come out with the most outrageous stories. I'd never had a lot to do with Billy up to that point, but I used to hear about his tales third hand.

So, I was relieved of hoist duties for a month and was under the tuition of Billy Bullshitter. It wasn't long before the tales started. Now what I'm about to write may well be true, I'll let you decide.

I told Billy my AA membership was coming up for renewal. No, I hadn't succumbed to the dreaded drink, it was the Automobile Association. The odd time I used to call them out, and I was always afraid to give the membership up. I used to think as soon as I gave it up the bloody car would break down somewhere. It wasn't that expensive, but this time I was stalling on it. In stepped, Billy.
'I don't have that problem, I'm a lifetime member.'
'Really? What did that cost?'
'Nothing. I wrote to them and told them I had a lot of AA memorabilia in my loft. They sent a guy to see me and he was amazed at my collection. He offered me money, but I said no. It's all on display at their headquarters in London. So, in gratitude, they gave me a lifetime membership. If you go there, Trevor, you'll see a plaque on the wall beside the display. "Kindly donated by Mr * ******."
Only Billy could top that story. I had a neighbour like him, Tony. I used to call him "Topper Tone." Didn't matter what I did, he had already done it, but obviously much better. It was only day two and it seemed like this was going to be a long month. He then topped the AA story.
'Did I tell you about the time I was on holiday in Devon?'
'No, I think you must have missed me out with that story.'
'Well the wife was happy just reading on the beach, but I wanted to do something. We had rented a nice little cottage opposite a church. So, one morning I wandered over and I bumped into the vicar. What a

nice man, getting on a bit in years. He told me he was sad to see the graveyard in such a sorry state. A lot of the headstones had moved because of subsidence over the years. I told him, don't worry about that vicar. I'll sort them out for you. So, the rest of the week I went around and straightened them out.'
'Christ, how many did you straighten?'
'About a hundred. I tell you, Trevor. When I finished the vicar came over, he was nearly in tears.
'Thank you so much **** he said."
'Another plaque?'
'What?'
'Just wondered if the vicar did something for you in return.'
'He mentioned about putting a stain glass window in with my name on.'

A story I was reminded of by Geoffrey Martin Smith is most probably my favourite.
Billy went to a concert in London. Before it could start an announcer came on the stage and said sadly the concert would have to be cancelled due to the conductor of the orchestra being taken ill. Unless of course there was anybody in the audience who had experience of conducting. Billy shot his hand up and he was invited onto the stage where he proceeded to conduct the orchestra with aplomb. At the end of the night, he was cheered to the rafters, so good, was he?

I'll stop here because I could fill this book up with his stories. I have an open mind regarding Billy. He did me a bad turn sometime later and I never forgave

him. We were in a busy period in the plant, it was the time when we had introduced temporary labour. Billy wanted to get his daughter a job, so he tapped me up. That was the nice part of being a steward, you could help get someone's family member get some temporary employment, often leading to a full-time job. So, I went to Human Resources as it was known by then and did the necessary. But, within weeks he had forgotten that good deed and did a bad thing behind my back. I found out, had it out with him and never spoke to him again.
Nothing as queer as folk.

Now a man who could give Billy Bullshitter a run for his money is Ian Shoulders, AKA, Stretch.
Now before I start, let me say I'm fond of Ian. He's a Facebook friend and a thoroughly decent guy.
Now the difference between Ian and Billy is Ian's stories, outrageous as they sounded, they were all true.
My favourite, his brother's wedding. Now before I start, for the benefit of people who don't know Ian, he has a certain way of talking. Not sure who started it, because there was another guy who worked with Ian for years, Steve Macklin who did the same thing. They'd finish a sentence with the word's "Yeah, Right." Or "You know what I mean?" Often, they'd say, "Yeah right, you know what I mean," all in one go!! Steve eventually left the company, moved down to Devon I believe. I think Ian was a bit heartbroken for a while, losing his buddy.
One morning he ambled into the Hoist crib.

'Alright Ian, wanna cuppa?'
'Go on then.' He plonked himself down and I could see he had something to tell me. A social call was rare from our Ian.
The conversation went something like this:

'Did I tell you my brother got married?'
'No, when was that?'
Saturday, a bloody disaster Trev, yeah, right.'
'Why, what happened?'
'Be quicker to tell you what didn't happen, yeah, right, you know what I mean?'
I made myself a cup of tea as well, I could feel Ian was going to be sitting there for some time.
I can't remember where the wedding was, it wasn't local because they were staying in a hotel somewhere.
'I told you my brother was marrying a girl from Canada, yeah right.'
'No, I don't recall you telling me that, Ian.'
'Doesn't matter, me and my brother stayed the night before the wedding in a hotel, yeah, right. We had a few beers and a laugh, you know what I mean?'
'I do.'
'Next morning, I get up, a bit worse for wear. Go down for breakfast and there's no sign of my brother? Right.'
'What's he done a runner?'
'What, no. Don't interrupt Trevor, yeah, right.'
'Sorry mate, carry on.'
'No, he's still in bed, yeah, right. So, I leave him to it, know what I mean?' This time I just nodded.

'I have a shower and I thought I'd better try me suit on, yeah. I'd not tried it on since I picked it up from Moss Bross, yeah.' So, I try the jacket on, yeah and the sleeves finish halfway up my arms, yeah right. The trousers I can't get up over me arse and the top hat is perched on the top of my head, way too small, yeah right.'

'Shit Ian, what did you do?'

'What could I do, Trev. I panicked, yeah, right. My brother's wife-to-be had about thirty relatives coming over from Canada for the wedding. There was me, the best man dressed like a clown, yeah. I went down to reception and asked for help. They told me there was a Moss Bross in the High Street. I take the suit with me and drive there, you know what I mean? Thank my lucky stars, yeah, right. They said they could change it free of charge. Job done, yeah, right, you know what I mean?'

'That was lucky, I mean, you are an odd size.'

'What do you mean, odd size?' Bless, Ian as a kid would have been called gangly. As an adult, he was known as that lanky bloke. (Amongst others) Ian towered over me, must be at least six feet four or five.

'I'm just saying, you're not the normal off the peg size, are you?'

'Yeah right. Doesn't matter. I had my suit and went back to the hotel. I just got back to my room, yeah, right. When there's a knock on the door. I open it, right, guess who's standing there, yeah?'

'Room service?'

'No, my brother. Wearing his suit, yeah right. One problem, yeah. The sleeves are way too long, the jacket is hanging off him, the trousers are about a foot too long and the hat is covering his eyes, you know what I mean?'
'I do Ian, you mixed up the suits.'
'Correct. How do you know that?'
'Call it a lucky guess, Ian.'
So, another ten minutes pass as Ian tells me about another mad dash to this famous "Moss Bross," which without asking him I assumed he meant Moss Brothers suit hire. Thinking he was giving his closing speech I stood up.
'Sit down, Trev. I haven't got to the best bit yet, yeah, right.'
'What there's, more?'
'More, you won't believe this next bit, yeah. We get ourselves ready, yeah, right. Drive to the church, yeah, right. Thought it was looking a bit quiet, just a couple of people standing outside. My brother tells me that's a couple from Canada. So, we walk into the church, right. On the left about fifty people, thirty odd, from Canada and the bride's friends. On the right, our family, or I should say where I family should be sitting. It's empty Trev, yeah, right.'
'Christ Ian, what did you do?'
'What could I do, Trev? I panicked, right.'
'Where were they?'
'I dunno. We have the bride's guests and family sitting there who have travelled over three thousand miles, and my lot who had to travel thirty miles and they weren't sitting there, yeah, right.'

‘What happened to them? I’ll tell you what happened to them, they were sitting in the wrong church, Trev, yeah, right.’
Well, I can’t remember the last time I laughed so much. You see it wasn’t just the funny story, it was the way Ian told me. He had this deadpan look and rarely smiled. Even when I was laughing he didn’t crack his face. It’s characters like Ian I really miss. He moved on to better things and I’m pleased for him. He ended up marrying our little electrician Amanda. Although there is a huge height difference, they always look extremely happy. Good on you guys.

I think what I’m trying to get across here is when you’re in a factory environment you come across a real spectrum of characters. I’m only scratching the surface of some of the people I met during my time at the plant.

I hit thirty, and I was not happy about it. I know you can’t stop the march of time, but I didn’t want to be thirty. It was “Live Aid” day. Everybody was watching the bands playing at Wembley Stadium and America. I was slowly getting depressed. Can that really be over thirty-two years ago? Oh well with age comes maturity. Really!!!
Enter a new foreman, Clive Gibson. We must have had a reshuffle, I have a feeling our dear foreman Ken was shipped down to Product Engineering. A good move for him in my eyes. I mentioned it before, he was too nice to be a foreman, so he was put out to see the rest of his time in a nicer atmosphere. I’d see

him occasionally, he looked a lot happier. So, Clive took us over and we soon discovered he didn't trust us? He couldn't help but check you were where you should be and the job was done. He was Australian, so we called him Skippy. An odd-looking man with his receding hair and "Amish" beard. He looked like he had his head on upside down. Now just as my luck went, Skippy moved to Maldon and became my neighbour! This became a problem because I had to drive past his house to get to mine. So, no sneaky off from work early for me. Not that I ever did! He had four kids and a wife called Mary. Now I met Mary a few times and she was a compulsive smoker and like Ian Shoulders, she often finished a sentence with the word, yeah. (A little side note here. I used Mary as a character in my first book "The Curry Affect.")

Now Skippy had bought a Ford Granada, he was one of these guys that would take on major repairs or upgrades. So, the Granada was soon in bits, strewn all over the front garden. He tapped me up for a lift to work.

'No problem,' I said. Secretly cursing away to myself.

I decided it was time for a bit of fun with our new foreman. It was the middle of the winter and bloody freezing. Skippy only ever wore a very lightweight jacket, more suited for summer. When I got home that evening I blocked off the heater pipe to my car. Next morning a came out of my front door looking like I was setting off on an arctic expedition. Thermal vest and long johns. Two pairs of socks. Jogging bottoms with jeans over the top. T-shirt, sweatshirt and a jumper. Woollen hat and gloves and a big

parka with a fur-lined hood. I put sunglasses on but felt that was a bit over the top so took them off. I had trouble walking, so I waddled around to my garage and got the car out. I pulled up outside Skippy's and he hopped out and into my car.
'Jesus H Christ, you feeling the cold?'
'Just a tad, Clive. Didn't I mention my heater has stopped working?'
'No, you didn't.' As Clive spoke you could see the mist coming out of his mouth. It was a thirty-minute drive to work, I guess we had been going about ten minutes before his teeth started chattering.
'You alright there, Clive?'
'Just feeling a bit nippy,' he replied with a shiver. The time we arrived at work he was a light shade of blue. He didn't wait for me, he just ran into the plant for a defrosting session.
The journey home that night he'd got himself a coat out of the stores. He was still cold, but not as much as he had been in the morning. I couldn't keep it up as I could hardly see out of the window screen. I had to keep scraping the ice off. So that evening I unblocked the pipe and in the morning, I had another bit of fun. I set the alarm clock fifteen minutes earlier. That gave me time to start the car and warm it up. I put the heater on full blast and by the time I pulled up outside Skippy's the car was roasting. I had my coat in the back seat and sat there in just my jeans and a t-shirt. Out stepped, Skippy. Looking like I did the day before, I don't know how many layers he had on, but he resembled the "Michelin man." He plonked himself in the car.

'Jesus H Christ, you could have told me you got the heater fixed.'

'I didn't know, Clive. It just started working. I hit the accelerator so he couldn't get out to strip off. He did manage to get his coat off, but I'm guessing the thermals were on and working because when I looked at him he was dripping in sweat ...... In January.

Not sure if he wanted revenge, or he'd heard about my zebra crossing skills, but he sent me down the hill to paint some yellow lines in another building down the hill. I'd used the machine before to paint lines, so not a problem. Now I should mention before I went off to do this job I had to report to the office with the others on my shift for a five-minute Health and Safety briefing. I'm guessing another directive from the Health and Safety guys. So, Skippy reads out the weekly Health and Safety Item. This week it concerned about miss use of tractors.

'They're not a taxi, so I don't want to see them parked outside the canteen.' Skippy was directing this at the wooden rubbish guys, it was only them and the gardener that drove the tractors in the plant. So off I go and soon knock the lines out. I wanted to get back for tea break so had a hurry on. I got to the bottom of the hill and was just about to push the machine up when a tractor pulled up. Terry Watts, one of the wooden rubbish guys poked his head out.

'Want a tow back?'

'Thanks, Terry.' I get behind his tractor and step on the tow bar. I have one hand holding onto the tractor and one hand hanging on to the machines handle. I must have looked a bit like a surfer, knees bent and hanging on for dear life. To be fair, Terry didn't go mad, he chugged along and before no time I was back in the main plant. Now unbeknown to me at that time was I'd been spotted by Skippy. Mark Clothier AKA Marky Mark. Now Mark will also feature later in the book. He came to see me after I had received a bollocking from Skippy.

'It was so funny, Trevor. Skippy was telling us that it was serious the Health and Safety briefing he'd mentioned in the morning when you came along standing on the back of a tractor hanging onto the yellow line machine.' Now Mark could do a wicked Australian accent.

'He just looked and said, "Jesus H Christ, I don't believe it, he's meant to be the health and safety rep."

I think it's fair to add that Clive wasn't best pleased with Terry and me. He would go on about cars all the time, I listened in when he reeled off a load of car part brands I'd never heard of. One, Mark reminded me of was Skip brown suspension? He talked the talk, but that Granada was in bits for months. By summer it was starting to be hidden by the long grass. Clive had a posh 4-bedroom detached house in a little close with only three other houses. I was a bit further along in my 2-bed semi. I did wonder what his neighbours must have thought about the front of his house. I bet they thought a traveller had moved in.

Talking about Skippy has reminded me about "The Tug Club." That was the name of our mobile video porn club. A few of us had clubbed together and bought a few porn videos. Now, this was the time when videos were at their peak. I won't mention the other shareholders .... Certain stories I will protect the guilty.

Marky Mark designed the membership cards, I printed off the film list and we got to work. We stuck some adverts up on the notice boards, and you could ring the wooden rubbish number and order a film. The advert made me laugh. At the bottom, Mark had put "Free Belly Wipe with Each Film." We used to have these blue paper towels in the toilets. So, we had a pack and when a film was ordered, it would go in a plain bag and a paper towel. Why Skippy reminded me about the video enterprise was he tapped me up for a free film one day.

'You're involved with this tug club, aren't you?'

'Couldn't say, Clive.'

'Listen, I've turned a blind eye to you driving around on your buggy delivering films.' I had a small electric buggy to carry the ladders and tools for my hoist work.

'Get to the point, Clive.'

'Mary's going away with the kids this weekend, thought I might get a film, au gratis.'

'You want a freebie?'

'You've got it.'

'I see what I can do.' On my travels, I go and see the boys and pick up a film that Marky Mark and myself thought would be perfect to him.

Not that I watched the film .... Well maybe once for quality control reason. The film starts off normal with

a beautiful blond and a guy at it. Soon to be joined by a third man who starts on the other guy. Not something us red-hot males like to see.
So, I popped it in the bag, slipped in the belly wipe and gave it to Skippy.
Monday morning, he marches in to see me.
'What sort of film is this?'
'Porn Clive, what you asked for.'
'But there are two men shagging each other.'
'Never.'
'There is I tell you. Jesus H Christ, I nearly vomited.'
'I watched the first five minutes, you sure?'
'Watch ten minutes and then you'll see.'
'Sorry mate, this is a new film. I'll get you another.'
'Don't bother, Mary's back.'

He did get me back, and he didn't do anything. I'd grown tired of trying to get past his house unnoticed. I sold my house and moved to Wickford. A few months later he moved. I was gutted, I loved Maldon and didn't really want to leave. Within months he followed suit and moved to a village called Southminster. I Guess his neighbours had a party and put the flags up when they saw the sold sign.

Poor old Skippy, he was a bit of a square peg in a round hole. He didn't last long. Ended up like Bomando, checking stock. He was too clever for stock taking. He told me that many times!! Last I heard of him he was working for Vauxhall at Elsmere Port.

The "Tug Club" ran for a couple of years then fizzled out. Too many of us involved. So not much profit and a pain having to deliver and pick up.

I should write about my two close working colleagues at this point. Johnny Manning, he became a good friend and a joy to work with. Well, that's when I could stop him talking and rolling a cigarette.
'Hang on, Trev. Let me just work up a bit of steam.' That was his favourite saying when he wanted to make a roll up.
I'd hated sending him off to get something. He was a bloody nightmare.
'Pop to the stores and get this, John.' Off he'd go, I'd carry on with the repair until I couldn't do anymore. I'd walk to the stores and there he was, talking. Often accompanied with a cup of tea in his hand. 'Just on my way, Trev.' My god, he could talk for England. I more laid-back guy I've never met. He operated at one speed, slow to moderate.' I've been to his house many times; his wife Molly and kids are a lovely family. Always made me feel welcome. John's house is lovely, decorated nicely and very homely. Not overloaded with ornaments and such like. Now, this surprised me because, at work, John was a hoarder. He hated throwing anything away. The Hoist workshop was on the move, we had to downsize. This was late in our time at the plant. Engine machining and assembly had all been ripped out. 70% of our spare hoists were obsolete, as were thousands of lifting hooks. We were told to get rid. There was only John and me working on the hoists.

I'd have a right old chucking out session. Next morning I'd come back in and half what I chucked was back? It got that bad I had to hide where I was throwing it.

For all his faults, John was a great guy to have as a work partner. Very good on a computer and always on hand to help. He knew I was strapped for cash for a time, he waited to see me and said, 'You do the weekends Mate, I've got no mortgage so I'm okay.' So, for a few months until I got myself straight he gave me his overtime. It tells you what a quality person John is. Unselfish and kind. He is one of the guys I miss the most from the plant.

Unfortunately, John's eating habits and smoking caught up with him. He had a heart attack in his mid-fifties. A serious one by all accounts. John's wife Molly phoned me and told me what had happened. Luckily in the Basildon area, they have a wonderful hospital with a top class cardiac department, fully manned 24 hours a day. John was literally wheeled off the ambulance and straight into the operating theatre where they fitted stents to his blocked arteries.

I told Molly I would pop in and see him after work the next day. Walking into his ward I expected to see him laid up fitted to machines. So, I was shocked when he walked over looking better than I'd seen him for a long time.

'He said something to me that I'll never forget.'

'I'm never smoking again.' He'd obviously had a visit from some doctor or another telling him he was in there because of his smoking. He looked well, I

couldn't believe he'd just had a heart attack. Luckily over time, John made a full recovery. I won't mention the smoking, John!
We still keep in contact and it's always a pleasure talking with him.

Now the other hoist man was Stephen Battle. AKA, Stevie as he liked to be called. I never called him Stevie, told him it sounded like a tarts name.
Now Steve must have joined us when he was in his mid-twenties. Fresh out of the army, he was lean and mean. Had a strong Birmingham accent. His claim to fame was his uncle on his mother's side was none other than rock star Roy Wood, of The Move and Wizzard fame. I teamed up with Steve when he was in his mid-thirties. By now the lean had turned to fat. Being a cider drinker was taking its toll on this once skinny man. Steve was one of these characters that if he took up something he'd give it his all and try and become the best. I can remember when he was trying to be a knight. He'd joined these bunch of people who dressed up at weekends and pretended it was 1066. He'd have the full metal suit and go into battle ... literally.
He took up golf and was playing every bit of spare time he had. I think he near enough became a scratch golfer. But he bored easy, he'd get good at something and that was enough for him. Although he was ex-army, it hadn't seemed to rub off in his personal cleaning habits. He wouldn't wear overalls at work. What he arrived in he worked in. He'd go out in the same clothes at night. For a while, he

adopted the string vest look. Jeans, string vest and his belly sticking out. The lads nicknamed him Onslow, from the character in "Keeping up appearances." I think Steve suffered a bit from dyslexia. Someone had written "Onslow" on his locker. He said to me.
'Why are they calling me Oneslow, Trev? I'm not slow, am I?'
I can remember Tony Lynch coming into our crib and telling Steve he must wear an overall jacket. Tony went back to the office as Steve stripped of stark bollock naked and just put his boots back on and the jacket. He marched into the office and shouted.
'Happy now?'
I can remember coming into work one day and I could smell horrible food. Steve and Tony Lynch were sat eating a bowl of soup each.
'We're on the cabbage food diet.' I think Steve lasted a few days. Tony Lynch did it for months. Not the plan that was in the book. Tony would eat it Monday to Friday. Then knock back about thirty Guinness's over the weekend. We were on opposite shifts but we used to see each other on the changeover. We'd work together some weekends and shutdowns.
One particular shutdown he brought in two pairs of funny buck teeth. They came with a putty that would mould them to fit perfectly over your own teeth. We had such a laugh wearing them. Shutdown period signalled a lot of contractors in the plant. These guys had no Idea the teeth were fake. We'd walk up to them and say, 'Excuse me mate, any idea where the toilet is?' They used to give us the double-take look.

Great fun. For some reason shut down signalled water fights. I have no idea why, but you'd go somewhere and someone would step out and launch a bucket of water over you? Of course, Steve and I decided to take revenge on anyone who dared to throw water at us.

'Not sure why, but I teamed up with two others to take on the Effluent Plant. They were situated at the bottom of the estate, away from everybody. I think they had sneaked up on us previously and given us a dowsing.

Joining me on the raid was Marky Mark and National Front, George, AKA Tripod.

We armed ourselves with the water style fire extinguishers, stripped naked apart from boots and dustbin bags covering us. We tiptoed our way there. We could see them up on the roof painting. Not one of our better ideas because we had to climb up onto the roof. Mark and I decided the best ploy would be to send George up.

'I don't know about that,' he complained.

'Just get up there George, we'll cover your back.' So, George made his way up this metal ladder and Mark and I stood ready. Before we knew it, we had been spotted. Some of the opposition had been working inside the building, had seen Mark and me and come out blazing a fire hose at us. Luckily, we legged it before the big fire hose came on. Unfortunately for George, he had to get back down on the ground. I looked back and could see George now running for his life. I'll never forget that vision of George being blasted by that fire hose. The bin bags had been

blown off and Mark and I watched as the full power of the water jettisoned him along the road.
'You pair of bastards,' he managed splutter out. Like I said earlier in the book, getting into your thirties comes with a bit more maturity.

Steve and Tony Lynch loved to have a sauna. We had one at work, attached to the gym. We weren't meant to use it out of hours, but we did. I went up there one night and Steve and Tony were sitting there with hair dye on?
'You pair of tarts,' I called out. I had a rather unsavoury sauna with Steve one night. We were both on nights for some reason, must have been a two-man job needed doing. For some reason, he talked me into having a sauna with him. I don't think he liked going up there on his own in the middle of the night.
So, we get there, switch it on and strip off. After a few minutes Steve picks up the bucket and empty's the contents on the heater. The smell of piss hit us like a brick. Some bastard had pissed in the bucket. Christ that smell stayed with me for days. To make matters worse because Steve didn't close the door on the way out the steam hit the fire alarm. Before we were dressed the alarm went off. We legged it pretty sharpish. It wasn't long before Roy Burton from security paid us a visit.
'You pair of clowns, I saw you scurrying away from the sauna.'
'Not us, Roy.'

'Yes you, I have you on the camera.' Luckily Roy was a friend, still is to this day. He wiped the film off for us. I've always said that Roy Burton is a gentleman!

Steve broke up with his wife, it was a traumatic time for him, and every poor sod that heard the story over the next few months. He told me he was going to kill himself. He had the shotgun pointed in his mouth and finger on the trigger. I know it was a really bad time for him and I tried to be supportive. Problem being he had to keep going on about it. We'd be out in the plant somewhere doing a job and he'll see someone and call them over.
'You heard I split up with, Chris?'
'No, Steve, I hadn't.'
'Yeah, nearly shot myself, I'd had enough. Had the barrel in my mouth, just couldn't pull the trigger.'

A month later:
'Alright, Dave. 'You heard I split up with, Chris?'
'No, Steve, I hadn't. I'm sorry to hear that
'Yeah, nearly shot myself, I'd had enough. Had the barrel in my mouth.' I had the finger on the trigger, but couldn't pull it.'

I couldn't take it anymore, I had an outburst.
'You mention the gun once more I'll pull the fucking trigger for you.' He sulked for a few weeks then we kissed and made up.
He soon was up and running again. His next-door neighbour was a nice guy who worked in the plant. John Castles, AKA, Forrest Gump.

We nicknamed him "Forrest" after we chased him through the plant in a car and couldn't catch him. It was amazing the speed people could run when they saw a guy with a fire extinguisher hanging out of a car window!

Anyway, John was married to a Canadian girl. I'm still friends with John now, He lives in Ontario and loves the Canadian way of life. I'm not sure if it was a relation of John's wife but Steve had started to write to this Canadian woman. A romance blossomed and he was smitten. He came into work one morning and told me he was having the following week off.

'I see, bit short notice isn't it.' Steve was all sympathetic, but basically, the woman was flying over to see Steve for a week's visit.

Now, Steve would never do anything by half. So, he hired a stretch limousine to take him to Heathrow and bring them back to Basildon. Now he used my friend, Lee for the limousine. I'd got Lee into the plant went they were taking on temps. He ended up doing the limo work part-time. So, Steve booked him and on the day in question, I received a phone call from Lee.

'You won't believe what happened at the airport.'

'What?'

'I took him, and he wanted me to stand next to him as I had the chauffeur's uniform on, so to make him look important. So, we're standing at arrivals, Steve's got a photo in his hand checking out any women that were on their own. His looking and this big old woman keeps blocking the view. In the end, Steve shouts at her, "Can you move please, I'm looking for my girlfriend." This woman turns around and shouts, Stevie.'

Well, I couldn't stop laughing. Lee told me he looked at the photo and then said to her, 'I take it this is a very old photo.'

Not one to kick a man when he's down, I waited a good two minutes after his week off and he returned to work. No one had seen him for the week. Tony Lynch had invited them both to dinner one evening but Steve cancelled last minute.

'Not like Steve to pass on a free dinner,' I remarked when Tony told me. I knew the real reason, but I kept it to myself.

Steve slumped in a chair looking all dejected.

'So, how was your week off?'

'Not good, Trev, not good at all.'

'Oh, sorry to hear that mate, did she not turn up?'

'No, she didn't. She sent someone who looked like her mother.'

He then proceeded to tell me the story.

'I'm sorry to hear that Steve, a whole week with her? What on earth did you do?'

'I only took her out in the dark. It's been the longest week of my life.'

It was around this time we were given a computer in the Hoist Crib. In the early days there was no restriction on the internet, so we could near enough go onto any site. This was all a bit alien to Steve, so he didn't get involved.

'You know what you should do.'

'What.'
'Get yourself onto the internet dating game.'
'You reckon?'
'Without a doubt.' I look at a well-known dating site and it starts showing some women in the Basildon area. Steve's eyes start to pop out.
'She's nice, that one's nice, look at her, she's nice.'
'Calm down mate.'
'She's nice, write to that one, Trev.'
'I can't, you have to join.'
'Sign me up then.'
'It's twenty-five pounds for a month.'
'Money well spent, Trev. Hang on.' He goes off to his locker and comes back with his bank card.
Next ten minutes we spend sorting out his personal details.
'Right they want to know your body shape?'
Steve stood up and tried to suck his belly in.'
'Average, Trev.'
'Interests?'
'Clay pigeon shooting, darts and golf.'
'You're going to be a real catch for someone, Steve.'
John Manning had turned up and showed us how to put a photo in his profile. He was up and running. Steve went home, leaving John and me to make some adjustments. I kept a note of his internet dating password, so we went back into his profile. John played around with the photo and somehow managed to take about thirty pounds off his weight and ten years off his age.
'That's better, John. We need to make him more interesting. Ten minutes later Steve Battle was a tri-

athlete, whose hobbies included fitness training, travelling, Ice skating, water skiing and mountain climbing. He'd run the London marathon in under four hours.

The next day I came into work on the late shift and Steve was smiling away.

'You'll never guess, I've had over thirty interests and eight messages of women wanting to meet me.'

'Never.'

It's true, Trev. I'm meeting one tonight.'

I must admit I did feel a tad bad, but it had gone past the point of no return. He went home a happy bunny and I logged into his account and put his profile back to what it was before.

The next afternoon I must admit I was a bit apprehensive, but a wave from Steve signalled normality.

'So, how did the date go?

'Not good. I waited outside the pub but she never showed up. In the end, I went in and I pulled the barmaid. Happy days, Trev.'

Steve eventually settled down with a lovely Irish girl called Catherine. I think her sister was married to Steve's cousin, something like that anyway. She came over from Ireland and lived with Steve.

Steve and I are the same age all bar a day. It would account for our similar sense of humour. One particular birthday he came in very happy.

'Happy birthday, Steve. What did Catherine get you?'

'A hang-gliding course.'

Now what I can say about Steve, he was a bit adventurous, a bit like the factory's version of Bear Grills.

A few weeks later he tells me he won't be working the weekend.

'I'm going to Sussex to do my hang gliding course.'

'Good luck with that, mate.' Now I must admit I did have my doubts. Steve was at his biggest, he must have tipped the scales at seventeen stone. But he was going to a professional flying outfit, so I didn't give it another thought.

Monday morning, I didn't need to ask Steve how it went. He came in and slumped in the chair. He didn't even spike his hair which was unusual. Many a morning he'd walk in, wet his hair and stick his hand in the sugar jar and rub it in his hair. But this particular morning, he just sat there. So, I made him a cup of tea and tried to coax the problem out of him.

'How was your weekend?'

'Disastrous.'

Oh, sorry to hear that. Hang gliding not go well then?'

'You could say that. I drove two hours to get to this place. Spend a whole morning watching videos, filling out insurance forms. Have to go outside and jump off a box to simulate a landing, there's only three of us on the course. We have lunch and then the problems start. First, they don't have a flying suit that fits me. I'm eventually squeezed into a suit that makes me look like Norman Wisdom. Then they pull these scales out and ask me to get on. I could tell there was a problem. Then this guy gets on a computer and starts to make calculations. This is followed by a lot of head nodding. Then they tell me. Sorry, Steve. But for you and our instructor to get enough speed to gain a lift off you'll need to be running at 42mph.'

'Shit mate, what happened?'

'Do I look like Linford Christie, Trev? What do you think happened, I came home.'

I must admit I did feel sorry for him, he'd had his wings clipped.

I went with him once to see his uncle Roy at the Cliffs Pavilion, Southend. I think he was billed as Roy Woods Big band at that time. Great concert and because of Steve's family connection we got backstage after and I met the great man himself.

Soon after, Steve was gone. His girlfriend Catherine owned a house in Ireland, I don't think she really settled in England. Things at work were changing, we had to do a lot more computer work associated with the job. Steve was computer illiterate and that spelt the end for him. He took a small package and waved goodbye.

I've never heard from him or heard anything about him since. It must be twelve years ago since he left. Like John, I miss him. In a perfect world, the three of us would organise a meetup, relive the story's and get drunk. However, I'm 6000 miles away and Steve is somewhere in Ireland. But the beauty of fond memories, no one can take them away.

Chapter 5

The rise of the foot soldier.

I felt the need to get to the next level within the Shop Steward committee. I'd done a number of years as a junior steward and felt it was the right time to make a move upwards. I was eyeing a JWC Position, being on the "Joint Works Council," was a prestige's position back in the day. Now my JWC steward was a guy called Eddie Edwards. Not the nutcase with the large glasses who jumped off snowy hills on skis. Our Eddie was a long-serving steward and well liked. However, I'd had a major set to with him and something had to give.

The trouble with Eddie, he'd grown weak over the years. It's something that can happen to a long-serving steward, you get a bit too comfortable. Basically, Ferris and Clemmie had him in their pocket. This was soon discovered by the *rat* when he was asked to pay Ferris and Clemmie a visit. You see the *rat* was now the convenor, so they asked him, not summonsed like the rest of us.

He sat and listened as Ferris and Clemmie put their case. They said it was ridiculous that Trevor Whitehead could be on the JWC. Eddie had served that position well for a number of years. Dave told me the conversation at a later date.

You see I was quietly confident I could take him out, I knew Eddie had backed George Catton when it came to the vote of no confidence. I had the convenors support, although he kept it to himself. I had great

help from the likes of Geoff and Alan Phillips, and from a steward who became a great friend. Tony Wilson. Now, Tony, today is a very successful man. I'm Facebook friends with his lovely wife, Pat. They have been happily married for over thirty years now. A bit like Ian and Amanda, Tony being well over six feet and Pat just about five feet nothing. His early beginnings as a steward you would have thought he'd come from a trailer park. Bermuda shorts, boots and vest. He must have used the same tailor as Steve Battle at the time. Despite this, he soon rose up the ranks did our Tony. Despite his looks in those days, Tony was well-spoken, sometimes to an extent, I'd thought he'd swallowed a dictionary. The *rat* kept on at him to smarten himself up, and eventually, he started to wear overalls. Through the *rat's* help and guidance, Tony was removed from being a final assembly worker to being transferred to the garage repair. Just by luck one day I was walking past and saw Tony standing by this brand-new toolbox on wheels and all these shiny tools inside. I'd not heard he'd been transferred, so it was a bit of a shock.
'Alright, Tony. What you got there?'
'I'm working in the garage now.'
'Really? They are going to let you loose on these expensive tractors?'
'What's wrong with that?'
'What's wrong with that? I had to come round and hang a pair of curtains for you. Now you're going to be repairing vehicles worth thousands of pounds?'
'Yeah, I know. Funny old world.' To be fair, and in case a farmer is reading this and about to blame our

Tony for his vehicle not starting. Tony never actually picked a tool up. It was just the *rat's* way of getting him off the line.

We became good friends and he was a great help getting me on the JWC. He'd seen the weakness in Eddie, it was time for the changing of the guard.

When I think back, Tony and I were lucky we didn't get fired one day. At the time, the store's foreman was a guy named Alan Morley. Now Alan was born in the wrong era. He would have been the ideal spiv back in the fifties. The pencil moustache and the greased back hair, the strut and the wide boy image.

The stores was located next to the convenors office, so Alan was a frequent visitor. He was a joker, loved to tell a tale and was always ridiculing the store's steward, the one and only "We're all going to get old and die," Paul Norris.

Now as previously mentioned, Paul is another ex-steward who went on to better things. In actual fact, now I'm writing about him, he deserves a lot of credit. Because when I first got to know Paul, he could barely do joined up writing. His spelling was littered with mistakes. I guess Paul felt like he'd won the lottery with the introduction of *spell check*.

Now, it was alright for us stewards to mock each other, but we were a solid team, if someone from the outside tried, they'd do it at their peril.

For a while, Alan would come in and take the mickey out of Paul, often when he was sitting there. He did it one day and it was the straw that broke the camel's back as far as Tony and I were concerned. Tony

suggested and I agreed to pay Alan Mortimer a visit on his own turf.
We must have looked like the Mitchell brothers on "EastEnders," only difference, we had hair. Marching into the stores, there was no sign of Alan.
Undeterred we entered Alan's office and proceed to tip his desk upside down. I can still remember the opened mouth look on the store's guys as we walked away.
Alan came after us, he'd lost face with his men. The *rat* made us go and apologise, which we did, half heartily.
Fair play to Alan, he could have reported us, but he was happy to see the pair of us apologising and kept it in-house.
The meeting to elect the JWC members was electric, you could feel the tension. Eddie had underestimated me, he'd also crossed the line by bad mouthing me behind the scenes.
Not a wise move. The *rat* was different to Bill Cleary. Where Bill wanted to be the mouthpiece and everybody else keep quiet, the *rat* wanted stewards who would speak up. I had a big mouth, so I knew I was his type of steward. Eddie couldn't give me eye contact, it was at that point I knew I was in with a shout.
So, with the help of a few trusted comrades, they did the paper ballot and by a small margin, I had won. To be fair to Eddie, he shook my hand and said well done. He took early retirement soon after. A good shop steward in his day, but things were changing.

Oh, I would have loved to be a fly on the wall when the news filtered through to Ferris and Clemmie. They'd lost their yes man, I was ready to do battle. Clemmie had been the manager for about seven years and I could count on one hand the number of times he'd spoken to me. He had no choice now. Really, I should ask Geoff and Tony what I was like back then. But then again, I might not like what they say. I know I had a spring in my step and was looking forward to rattling a few cages.

Unfortunately, I never really got stuck into either of them, within a month they'd both retired. I couldn't believe it. I was happy to see the back of Clemmie, he'd kept a tight rein on any overtime. Must have been his Scottish heritage. I could have written that once I was an elected JWC member they ran for the hills, but this is not a fictional book.

Now, a strange thing happened next. For some reason, whoever had divvied up the constituency's many years previously decided that the JWC position that I now held, meant that I now represented the security and fireman as well as a host of others. I did know a few of them, and at the start, I had little to do with them. They had their own steward, Roy Wood. Nice guy, polite and unassuming. Not sure exactly what happened, but Roy decided to quit. The *rat* put a notice up for a replacement. Unfortunately, as it turned out for me, no one stood.

The *rat* called me over to his office and explained that they must have a steward. As nobody would volunteer, I'd have to take on the role, after all, I was their JWC member he explained.

'You can't cherry pick, Trevor. Besides, there's only a few of them, a piece of cake.'
It didn't take long for me to be choking on the said cake.

So, an introduction meeting was arranged. I was a bit apprehensive as what I knew about security and firemen you could write on a back of a matchbox! For the life of me, I can't remember what went wrong at the first meeting with the Security chief, a big white-haired, red-faced man called Jim McClure. I'd never spoken to the man before. But he wanted to meet me and a time was for a meeting was set. Now big Jim had a number two, George Salmon, I soon discovered he was Jim's spy. I seem to recall I had organised a ballot about something or another, most probably overtime linked as this was always a touchy subject. I'd heard a rumour about them picking their favourites to do overtime more regularly than the others. Something I was keen to stop. Unbeknown to me, Jim didn't like my interference. He and George ran their own ship, how dare I hold a ballot without their knowledge. Oh, these pair were in for a rude awakening. How dare I interfere with their overtime choice. So, I turn up at the outer office where a couple of the guards were.
'Through there Trev, and good luck.' My god, you could actually see the fear in their eyes? I go to the office door and knock, then walk into the hub centre of security. Monitors everywhere and all sorts of equipment.

Funny how some things stick in your mind. Jim McClure's greeting being one of them.
'Think yourself lucky we let you in here. We have a strict rule about letting civilian's in here.'
What a cock, civilians? I took an instant dislike to the pair of them and it didn't take long to light the blue touch paper. The problem I had, I was unprepared. The previous steward, Roy Wood was off sick with stress, so I couldn't get any pointers from him. In hindsight, I should have maybe gone in with a different approach. Jim had always had one of his own as a shop steward, and by the looks of it, he had him in his pocket, so to him, I was a bit of an alien. I won't be far out when I recall the very brief first meeting.
'Civilian? I'm not a civilian, I'm the man you have to deal with now when you fuck up. And next meeting I want a cup of tea waiting for me. Where're your manners?'
Jesus Christ, I kid you not. I thought Jim's head was going to blow up. Already red, I could see the veins in his forehead popping.
'Do you know who you're talking to?'
'Yes, the so-called manager of security. And who the fuck are you?' I pointed at George Salmon.
'This is George, I've asked him to be here.'
'Well next time you want to bring a sidekick in, you ask me first.' People may read this and think I was a bit over the top. But I'd done my research. I had my own source of information inside the security. I won't reveal who because I don't want to embarrass him. But he remains a friend to this day. He'd told

me all about the way this pair treated the men. Well, as the great singer-songwriter Bob Dylan would sing. "The times they are a-changin". Plus, what could they do to me, I didn't work for them, I was in a win-win position. I think it's fair to say the next five minutes were spent hurling insults at each other. George Salmon tried to get in but I pointed at him and told him to shut the fuck up.
At some stage, Jim had picked up the sheet of paper that held the ballot result and ripped it up. In the end, I walked out. The security guards who wished me good luck were still hovering in the outer office. I think it's fair to say I'd gone up a notch or two in the eyes of these guys after that performance.
'Well, that didn't go to bad,' I said as I walked out. A few days later I had to accompany the *rat* to the Human resources where an attempt was made to smooth things out with Jim.

Once again it didn't take long to kick off again. It was obvious to everybody at the meeting that Jim and George didn't want me interfering in the way they run things. They wanted to control who worked overtime, something they had done unfairly for years. The *rat* soon backed me up and eventually, they had no option but to concede. It ended with a limp handshake and a new meeting was arranged.
I turned up and as I sat down, George Salmon asked if I took sugar. He most probably spat in it, but hey, a victory is a victory.

It wasn't long before this handful of men started to give me problems. I started to receive mail through the internal post. Pages and pages of complaints, I sat in amazement reading some of these letters. Four or five of them had written to me, telling me all sorts of stories, where I was going wrong, watch out for so and so. How this was unfair, how that should be changed. It soon became apparent that these guys had too much time on their hands. I did feel for these guys, they'd been treated badly by Jim and George, or Batman and Robin after I renamed them for years.

I'm not going to knock the previous shop steward Roy Wood. It is more difficult when you work for the man you're taking on. But, Roy and his predecessors had been in Jim's and George's pocket. It didn't take long for me to sort out Jim's spy.

I was in the convenor's office doing something and a fireman had spotted me. Now, these guys had not had someone speaking up for them for a long time. So, they had plenty to gripe about. I didn't mind and I would help when I could. Now this fireman was a really nice guy, he had a genuine problem and wanted some advice.

'You got a minute, Trev?'

'Sure, what's up? Well while this guy is asking me something, George Salmon walked in and started to bollock this guy in front of me.

'Who gave you permission to leave the job? You need to clear it with me and request a meeting with the steward.'

Now, technically that was true. But I wasn't having this man throwing his weight around. I grabbed him by his tie.
'Hang on George. Don't come into this office without knocking. Secondly, if you ever embarrass one of my members again I will personally take you round the back here and beat the living daylights out of you. Now fuck off.'
'Did you hear that, he threatened me.' Cried out a shocked George.
'I didn't hear anything,' smiled the fireman.
'Trust me, George. You ever pull a stunt like that again, you'll live to regret it.'
'Jim will hear about this.'
I hope not, George. Close the door on the way out.'
What a jumped up horrible man.

I have to say I found the security and fireman an odd bunch. They had some strange ideas, and I found that I had to be very careful what I said to them. They could recite something I said a year ago. I might say something to a couple of them and they'd say ....
'You've changed your tune. Last November when I spoke to you in the foyer, you remember, when you were going home, you said such and such.'
Unbelievable.

Now, the following incident you'll read, and you'll think I've exaggerated the story. But word for word this is true. After you read the following you'll have some idea what I was up against with these security

guards. Again, let me add, some of these guys were great, but some were complete morons.
I was working away in the Hoist Crib when Tony Lynch came and spoke to me.
'Get your arse down to Thurrock, there's a major problem with the security down there. You can take the security pool car.' Oh well, I thought this will kill a couple of hours. Now the Thurrock depot was some eighteen miles away. It was basically a packing place. Can't remember how many worked there, but maybe a hundred odd. The security was made up of current and a couple of contractors. Now, the two contract guards were ex-company guards. They had worked there for years and some deal was struck so they could retire, then come back working for a contractor. I'm trying not to muddy the water here by over explaining why there were some contract guards. It will become clearer later.
So, I drive to Thurrock, wondering what the hell this major problem was. So, I parked up and strolled over to the guard house. I was welcomed by "Little Shit." I won't use his real name. His nickname says it all.

'So, what's the problem?'
'I'll tell you the problem, look at that?' He opens a fridge and gives me a half-used carton of milk.
'What's this?'
'That's my milk, Trevor. And this guy has been using it to make his tea!'
Now, the guy he's pointing to is one of the contract guards. A man who only a few weeks previously had

been his shift partner before he took early retirement.
'You are joking with me I hope?'
'I'm not joking with you; this man is a thief.' It didn't take a rocket scientist to work out that little shit had a grudge against this man and had been waiting for him to slip up.
I was a bit flummoxed for a minute, I wasn't sure how to react. It was the contract guard that put things into perspective.
'I hold my hands up, Trevor. I did use the milk a couple of times in my tea, but it's not like we pay for it.'
'What?'
'No, the canteen slips us a few cartons every couple of days, bless them. We help them out with the delivery's.'
I turned to little shit.
'Let's get this perfectly clear. You've made a song and dance about some missing milk that was taken by a former work partner of yours. Milk that you didn't even pay for?'
'It's the principle, Trevor.'
I won't write what my response was, I'll leave you to imagine what was said.
See, I told you you'd think I had exaggerated. I kid you not, that is a true story.

The reason there were contractors helping out was that the security had been outsourced to another company. I don't want to run ahead of things so that unsavoury business has yet to come.

I guess I'm at the right stage in the book to bring in the other village idiot. Come on down, *Pat Brown*, the time is right.

Pat Brown worked and represented the engine side of things. Five minutes in his company and you'd wonder if the shop stewards committee were participating in "It's a Knock-out." Our younger readers won't remember that show, but it was fun to watch, and at any particular time you could play your joker. Enter Pat Brown.

The first time I met Pat I thought he was going out to rob a bank. He looked like he had a stocking covering his face, it took me a while to realise that was his natural look. Obsessed with the German's, it wasn't long before I named him *Pat von Brown.*

Even more amazing was the fact that Pat was not only a shop steward, he was a JWC member too. He'd taken over from George Sharpe who had retired. Sadly, George passed away not long into his retirement. It's a bitter blow when that happens, you work all your life and your time is cut short. His son Andy still works at the plant. So much like his dad, it's uncanny. Around the same time, we lost another shop steward, Dave Edwards, or Rupee Edwards as he was known amongst us stewards after a reggae singer. A smashing guy, too nice to be a steward really. I can always remember he called the gym …. Gyminasium?

'You off to the gyminasium then, Trev?'

'I am, Dave.' I never corrected him.

Back to Pat. Before I renamed him, Pat was known as Postman Pat. He had been given this name for good reason. Once in a blue moon, we would have a fire drill. It was always hush-hush so it made it more realistic. The whole plant had to empty and you had to get out into the carpark where your particular evacuation monitor would tick your name off. So, once we got back to work a whisper started about the count up. Everyone was accounted for, except one person.
I guess with Pat's face, he'd never be known as "Lucky." But what are the odds on you slipping out to the Post Office at the same time as a major evacuation drill? The company went mad with Pat. I think the *rat* had to calm things down. I'm sure Pat had a few days suspension over the incident.

Another Pat Brown classic was when he'd hurt his ankle. He hobbled into the convenors office limping. It will remain anonymous the two men who suggested they'd fake an accident for Pat. Someone came up with the bright idea of spilling some oil on the stairs that led up to the toilet. So, they made Pat sit at the bottom of the stairs and phoned the medical. The buggy with the stretcher attached arrived and whisked Pat off to the medical. Someone from the company health and safety came and looked at the accident scene. I think they suspected some form of foul play. Rumour has it that Dennis Morley arrived at the medical to check on Pat before he was taken off to Basildon Hospital. A shoe inspection was done and Pat's shoes were confiscated and Dennis locked them away. Not a drop of oil on them. The anonymous men hadn't thought the plan through.

A Christmas meal and drink up for the JWC members was arranged at Boreham House. This was a huge mansion type building, used for all sorts of things. It was my first chance to meet my new manager, Keith Davies. Over a few drinks, he told me his goal was to be Plant Manager. He was a lightweight in the drinking department and his wife turned up to take him home.
This night out with the JWC and management later became known as "Fedoragate."
The day in question, the *rat* turned up looking like Malcolm Allison, a football manager who was flamboyant and would often be seen smoking a cigar and wearing a Fedora hat. The *rat* wore the hat and it was his pride and joy. As the drinks flowed things started to get out of hand. The *rat* had unwisely left the fedora on the bar. Sorry, Geoff, I'm not taking all the blame for this one. Between Geoff and me we started filling the hat with all sorts, beer crisps, cigarette butts, the drunker we got, I think the worse the hat got abused. At some point, Geoff and I saw some sort of sense and did our best to clean the hat up. Basically, I washed it out with beer and stuck it on a radiator to dry.
A few hours later we piled onto the minibus, the *rat* was the last to get on. He was worse for wear.
'Hang on driver, I've forgotten my hat.'

'No, you haven't, I've got it here.' Geoff threw the *rat's* hat to him and he put it on his head. Unfortunately, a decent Fedora doesn't take kindly to being abused. The hat had shrunk and was perched high on the *rat's* head.
'What have you done to my hat, Geoff?'
'It wasn't me, it was Whitehead.'
'I never did thank you for dropping me in it, thanks, Geoff. Well, we headed back to Basildon and all the way the rat was whinging and whining.
'Cost forty-five pounds this hat, it's ruined.' The *rat* was lashing Geoff then me.
'Expected better of you, Geoff.'
'Nothing to do with me. I told you, it was Whitehead.' I could take no more. I grabbed the hat off the *rat's* head and threw it out of the window.
'There, fuck the hat.'
To be honest I can't remember much more about that night. For some unknown reason, the driver didn't drop us home, but in the company Club. I vaguely remember standing there with a beer wondering what the hell I was doing.
Of course, the next day at work the Fedoragate scandal was red hot news.
The funny thing now, as I think back. It was only a hat. The way the *rat* was going on you'd have thought I'd launched his pet dog out the window. Poor *rat*, he couldn't believe two of his trusted stewards could behave that way. The hat to him was another status symbol. A vainer person I've yet to meet. He was beyond insecure. He started to dye his hair and moustache, it made him look odd, with his

pale skin and jet-black hair. He'd walk into the canteen in the morning and chat one of the canteen women up for a free packet of cigarettes. He was a big lump *rat*, maybe six two and thickset. He sauntered over and sat with some of us stewards, it was a bit of a morning ritual. We'd have a cuppa first thing before heading off to various locations. This particular morning, he looked a cock, and I told him.
'What the fuck have you done to your hair?' It was the blackest I'd seen it. A grey hair or two must have surfaced on his moustache and eyebrows because they'd been dyed the same colour. I think I used to get egged on by Alan Philips, he was the *rat's* deputy. A fantastic character and loved the banter. As the *rat* was getting his morning freebie packet of fags, Alan set me up.
'Trevor, look at the state of his hair?' I take a look and when he sits down I have a little dig.
'Bloody hell. What have you done to your hair? I'm a friend, so I'll tell you. You look a c*** mate. Grow old gracefully.'
I think Alan and myself would have made a good double act because he would set me up, then come out with something like this.
'Oh, listen to Whitehead. That's a nasty thing to say. It looks good.' Of course, the *rat* loved his ego rubbed.
He had a real issue about his penis size. As I said. He was a big lump, but he had insecurities about his manhood. He had a heart to heart with me one day on how he thought women would think he'd be big in that department because of his body size. I'm not

sure I was the right person he should be talking to. I mean, I wasn't the most sympathetic of people.
'I see, so has someone complained then?'
'No, of course, not. I'm just saying, I wonder if they expect something a bit bigger.'
'Yes, I can see your point. You strip off and your little penis is poking out.'
'It's not little, it's average.'
'Depends on what you mean by average?'
'I mean it's normal size.'
'What's normal?'
'Well let me tell you, I've had no complaints.'
'They're not going to say anything, some woman like a small todger, so I wouldn't worry about it.'
'I haven't got a small todger.'
'Yes, you have, I caught you in the shower that time.'

The colouring of his hair reached new ridicule heights when we were outside for some meeting or another. I can only liken it to an episode of Dad's Army. The one where they Private Frazer, the Scottish undertaker tries to make them look younger. It works until they are parading outside and it starts to rain, causing all the hair colouring to run down their faces. Well, I'm not sure if the *rat* had used a cheap brand, but it started to rain and he befell the same outcome. One of the few times I nearly felt sorry for him.

I'm being careful what I write about the *rat*, he was a one-off, a convenor who in my opinion grew to be a monster. But in those early years, he was good at his job. He became the butt of many of our jokes. He

couldn't handle me, he used to complain about my lack of respect to the other stewards.
He'd bring a lot of my one-liners on by himself, aided by the ever wind up merchant, Alan Phillips.
Many a time Alan would kick it off. I walked into the office one day and Alan was sitting with the *rat.*
'Here, Trev. **** was just telling me he went out last night and was chatted up by a lovely looking blonde.'
'Fuck sake, you still hanging around that old age people's home?'
Another time.
'Trev, *** been telling me how he resembles Engelbert Humperdinck?'
'Really? I'd say more like Elvis on the day he died.'

When I think back to this period, I guess it was my golden years. The best is yet to come in this period, but let's get back to work.
Now, after security had eventually settled down I then got sidetracked by another mob. The air tool crib. Now I should say I'm still friends with two out of the four. The other two went mad. Maybe I'm a tad unkind as one of them did end up in the hospital with some mental health issues. The other became a foreman. Now to be fair, they were good trade union supporters and good supporters of me. I did wonder why they used to play up. They were on a good thing. If that was me I would have kept my head down.
How they managed it remains between them and the manager at the time. But they were getting three shifts pay for working a double day shift. So, they were extremely lucky. But for some reason, they

were always complaining about something, I have a feeling I might get some contact from two of them after they read this. But, I'm afraid to say the four of them were the classic example of the many backstreet lawyers we had in the plant.
I won't bore everybody with their numerous complaints, it got so bad once I had to bring the union's district officer in. They'd quote things from all different sources, Internet researched they'd hit me with all sorts. With these guys and security, it was a wonder I didn't go mad too.

Christmas time was always fun at work, a few freebie dinner invites, I think Boreham House had sent a message to the Plant Manager asking that the JWC have a Christmas bash at another place in future. We'd always try and raise some money for a local handicap school during the festive season. The stewards would man the gates and we'd embarrass a few pounds out of the workforce. Later in the morning, we'd go around the offices catching the staff. One-year sticks in my mind. Tony Wilson and I were tasked to go around the offices.
'Take George with you,' ordered the *rat*. Enter another George, *George Payne*.
Now, George was no village idiot, he just spoke like one. He regularly got his words mixed up. George was a good runner, he'd done a few marathons. I had not long got into running and had the London marathon on my bucket list. Some lunchtimes I'd join George, along with a guy called Greek George and another good runner Tony Baker. They'd set off and

I'd try and keep with them. We didn't run far, normally 5k. One day it was just me and George, and I made a big mistake trying to run his legs off. Now George was giving a good twenty plus years away to me, plus he carried a bit of weight around the middle. This particular lunchtime he said, 'You take the lead and I'll run along at your pace.' "Run along at my pace," I thought. Cheeky bastard. I had been running well (Or so I thought) So I set off, steady for the first kilometre, then I started to pick it up. By the fourth Kilometre, I was a spent force, reduced to a gentle jog. George shot past and I never saw him again until I staggered back into work and he was coming down from the locker room, changed!!
'What, you fall over.'
'Didn't want to embarrass you, George.' Lesson learnt that day. "Never judge a book by its cover."
So, Tony, George and I set off to the admin office block. These people we didn't really know. Occasionally I'd recognise someone from the cricket, but on a whole, they were complete strangers. I won't use the word intimidation, but we didn't let anyone escape the bucket. I chased a guy in the toilet once. Tony and I were old hands at this game, I let Tony and George hold the bucket and I'd watch for runners. You'd always get the odd tight arse trying to dodge the bullet. I watched one make a dash for the toilet.
'Give me the bucket,' I demanded as I closed in on this man. He thought he was safe, locked into one of the cubicles. I went into the cubicle next-door, put

the lid down, climbed up and hung over with the bucket.
'We're collecting for the children at Elmbrook School, Sir. Would you like to contribute?'
There were three or for portacabin offices outside the admin.
'Come on George, get in there with the bucket.' Tony passed George the bucket and we stood back. Now I'm not sure if the door was just stiff or they'd seen us and locked it. But George couldn't get the door open. This caused great amusement to Tony and me.
'Come on, George put your back into it.' George tried his hardest and the door wouldn't budge.
'For fuck sake George, let the dog see the rabbit.' I could see people in the office and they weren't escaping the bucket. I tried a shoulder charge and bounced back.
'See, let's leave it.' Suggested George.
'Needs a bit more persuasion, George.' I took a run up and the door flew in with me attached to it, straight off the hinges.
I'm crumpled up on top of the door which is now on the floor, frame as well. This seemed to take the wind out of George and when spoke it came out something like this.
'Collection school we are Elmbrook, contribute like bucket the children?' I stood up, the whole office was in a stunned silence. We decided that this time they could escape the bucket.
As predicted, my manager, the Plant manager in waiting, Keith Davis was shipped out. It's funny because I hadn't had a lot to do with him up to that

point. Keith had a clerk who became my best friend. *Steve Jarvis*. Steve used to worry about Keith Davies and me.

'Tread careful, Trevor. He is not a man to forgive easy.' Well, I never had a lot of time to test this out as one day I came in and Keith was gone. So, a new manager was appointed, one *Michael Newman*. Now, Michael wasn't everybody's cup of tea. But out of all the managers, I had before and after, Michael was the only one I liked. He was a very fair guy. He'd worked his way up to that position from the tools, like a few others, but he never forgot his roots. He was always willing to negotiate with me. First impressions you'd think he was a solemn man and very serious. He wore these half-rimmed glasses and when I had meetings with him, they'd be perched at the end of his nose. Dry sense of humour, and behind the scenes he was a nice guy. Michel will feature later on, as I feel it's time to get to the Tony Lynch era.

Chapter 6

A born comedian.

I can't remember how many foremen I had over a thirty-six-year period. Some were insignificant, some stood out, but one was in a league of his own. Tony Lynch, a born comedian if I ever met one.

He turned up one day out of the blue. I think it was the time we started the three shifts and he was transferred from being a production General foreman to a normal Forman in maintenance. To be honest I didn't have a lot to do with him in his early years. He was on a different shift to me, so only if there was a problem and the steward was needed would we communicate.

Tony was Irish, and he looked Irish. I think I mentioned earlier in the book that he reminded me of the great Irish comedian, Dave Allen.

He liked a beer did our Tony, and many a late shift he would pop down the Irish club for a quick pint or two. Jolly told me a funny story about him once when he was trying to sweep the office out after Tony had returned from his liquid late shift lunch. Tony was leaning against some filing cabinets and as he went to move out of Jolly's way both feet shot up in the air. As previously mentioned, it didn't take much to get Jolly in hysterics. Tony needed a hand up but Jolly was on all fours laughing hysterically and incapable of helping him. As time went on, and we reduced in numbers, we were left with two foremen to look after us. Tony and a nice guy Paul Wellstead. They became

known as Ugh and Wah. You'd go into the office and ask them something and Paul would just grunt. 'Ugh.' Followed by a Tony, 'Wah.' Which I took as a shortened version of What?
I've already mentioned the Tony Lynch weight loss programme. Cabbage soup Monday to Friday followed by a weekend of Guinness. He loved a gamble on the horses, and he'd always book the Cheltenham week off.
Paul liked a bet, but he was a dog man. Now, I'm not sure if Paul had a problem at some point with gambling. He never mentioned it and I certainly wasn't going to ask. But his wife kept a tight control on his purse strings. He was on good money, but he never had a lot on him at any time. His dog betting was only small amounts. He was a secret smoker too. Before he went home, he had a ritual of washing his face and hands and popping in a chewing gum.
'Surely your wife can smell the smoke on you?' I asked him once.
'She does, but I blame you guys.'
It didn't take a lot of working out who wore the trousers in that house. After Tony retired, Paul came into his own. He was a nice guy to have supervising you. Let you get on with things and always spoke to you in a civil manner.
Unlike Tony, who had a touch of Tourette. Tony and I had a good foreman/steward relationship. I have already told the story of the Stannah chairlift saga with Marky Mark and Jolly. I had trouble working out if he was serious about the incident. To be fair to the guy, he quit smoking and that is no easy task.

I was working on a hoist out in the factory one day and an operative asked me a question.
'What's he like your foreman?'
'Who?'
'Scissors.'
'Scissors, who the hell is Scissors?' Then the penny dropped, he was talking about, Tony.
You see Tony would stand out in an aisle way, legs apart, hands tucked in the back of his trousers with his elbows jutting out.
"Scissors," I loved that name for him.
I have many stories about Tony. His two favourite words were "Wah and Kunt."

I was working on a late shift, it must have been around the summertime as it wasn't getting dark until around nine. I'd had my dinner and was checking a hoist when "Bones" called me in a panic.
Now "Bones," was AKA Mark Lewin. Another guy and good friend Bob Fellows christened him Bones and the name stuck the rest of his working life. Mark was short and skinny. He'd been transferred to our department and ended up working with Bob and me for a while. We didn't get off to the best of starts. We'd been working inside a big wash machine. It was hot and sticky. We'd finished the job and Mark had gone off to get something. I climbed out and proceeded to wipe the grease off my hands on a bit of rag. I chucked it in the dustbin and Mark returned minus his shirt.
'Christ that was warm in there.'

'It certainly was, anyway it's all done now,' I announced.
'Great, shall we have a cuppa?'
'Good idea.' I start to walk off and Mark calls out to me.
'Trev, you seen my shirt?'
'Can't say I have mate.' I walk back and help him look. What colour is it?'
'Yellow.' I search around and can't see it.
'Strange, where could that have gone?' Mark then spots the yellow "rag" in the dustbin. Pulls it out and holds it up.
'You C***.' Not the best of starts!

Anyway, Bones is in a panic.
'I need help, Trev. You used to do yellow lines, didn't you?'
'Long time ago, Mark. Why what's up?'
'Best if I show you.' So, we amble outside and by the entrance to the factory was a large yellow lined cross hatch square, painted to warn people not to park there. Now, this crosshatch had been painted a number of years, occasionally repainted when it had faded. Tony Lynch had instructed Mark to freshen it up. Now, this crosshatch had been painted with two-inch-wide lines. When we get there, I see a mess.
'What the fuck, Mark. What have you done?'
'I tried to paint it by hand, but it's not straight.'
Basically, Mark had painted three sides of the square and the lines were all squiggly.
'Where's your string?'
'String? What do I need string for?'

'To keep the line straight, you muppet.' We go off and get some string. The time we get back, it's just starting to get dark.
'We need to straighten these three out.' I helped Mark but because of the squiggly lines, to get them straight, the line has gone from two inches wide to six. We just about finish the third line as the darkness beats us.
'You'll have to finish it off tomorrow, Mark. You've made a lot of work for yourself now.'
'No problem, it will look good the time I finish it.'
'Well make sure you use the string in future.'
'Will do, thanks, mate.' I walked off and thought no more about it.
Next afternoon I'm walking in and I see Tony in his "Scissors" position talking to Bones. Spotting me he called me over in his normal polite way.
'Whitehead, come here.'
Now Tony would sort of pull a gurning type of face when he was angry and close one eye. I can liken it to a "Popeye" look.
This is word for word how the conversation went. Bones stood there bemused.
'Tell me something, would you pay some kunt, eighty punds to paint tree yellow lines?' Because of his closed eye, I wasn't sure who he had directed the question at.
'You asking me?'
'Yes, you Kunt, I'm not asking this stupid kunt, am I?'
'Eighty pounds for three yellow lines?' I did the maths in my head.

'That's a tad over twenty-six pounds a line, yes, sounds a bit steep.'
'A bit steep, yer a kunt, Bones. And while I'm at it, why the fuck have you made them so big?'
'Just bringing them up to Government standard size, Tony.'
Mark had obviously had time to prepare his answers.
'What Government standard size.?'
'I went out and measured a few.' Mark tried to keep a straight face.
'Yer lying kunt, Bones.' Another one of Tony's quips he would use if he thought you were skiving. This lovely little sentence he would use regularly.
'You've been fucking the dog, Bones.' What a charming saying.
'Now fuck off and get those lines painted.' Mark walked off feeling lucky. Tony turned to me.
'These kunts will have me smoking again. He walked off, ready to throw a few more expletives at the next poor unsuspecting soul.

One thing that the guys liked about Tony was he would go out and seek overtime, it didn't matter how bizarre the task, he'd always agree to get it done. Whether it be clearing up the devastation left behind by the famous hurricane of 1987, where a group of us were sent to Boreham house to help clear up the mess. Jim Ferris was still with us then. He came over and said to four of us, 'Come on I'll treat you to a pub lunch.'
We walk across the road to a nice little country pub. Unfortunately, because of the storm, the pub had no

power. Oh well, we did get a bottle of warm beer and a packet of pork scratchings!

Tony called Marky Mark into the office on a Friday. 'Right you pair of Kunts, I have a special job for you the weekend.' It transpired Tony had agreed to get the fire station's big yellow door painted.
So, Saturday morning, armed with a couple of paint brushes, a paint roller and a tin of yellow paint, we amble up the hill to the fire station. Luckily, Roy Burton was on shift, so we're soon chewing the fat over a cup of tea.
After a while we decided to make a start, fearful that Tony would show up in the little Lancia estate car he used to drive around. Looking at the door, it looked a big job. But we soon knocked it out in less than thirty minutes.
'You lads want another cup of tea?' Not the sort of question you need to ask two professional tea drinkers. So, we get comfortable and Roy kept us watered. I look out of the window of their office and I see Tony pulling up in his car.
'Hey up, Mark. Stand by your bed, Lynch's just pulled up.'
Now, one thing I knew wouldn't happen, I knew Tony wouldn't be getting out of the car. He never did, so it was no surprise when he pressed and held the hooter.
The pair of us walked out, and the electric window comes down.
'Yer pair of kunts, yer fucking the dog.'

'Whoa …… Easy with the insults.' I was used to Tony's colourful language.
'We're not fucking the dog, if you must know, we're waiting for the paint to dry.'
'Paint to dry, you kunt.'
'Yes, we thought we'd give it another coat.' Tony sat there with a bemused look on his face then decided we could be doing something else, while we waited for the paint to dry. This, of course, we had no intention of doing.
'Follow me.'
I walked around the car and tried to open the passenger door. It was locked? Tony slid the window down about two inches then hollered at me.
'Walk, yer lazy kunt.' Mark and I had great trouble trying not to laugh. So, Tony started to drive slowly and the pair of us walk alongside the car. He had his window still down and occasionally he would shout something out.
'Pick that up, get rid of that, sort those weeds out, that shouldn't be there.' The problem for Mark and myself was that Tony had now speeded up, so we're now having to jog to keep up with him. We must have looked a right pair of clowns trying to keep up with him. Eventually, we stopped running, Tony by now was about fifty meters ahead of us. We could see the brake lights and then the reversing lights.
'Here he comes,' I muttered. However, Tony stopped about twenty meters from us. Stuck his head out of the window and shouted out his opinion of us.
'Yer pair of kunts and lazy bastards, wankers.' With that, Tony drove off. Mark and I took a good ten

minutes to stop laughing. The lovely thing about Tony, the incident was never mentioned again. As we walked back to the fire station we wondered if we had time to squeeze another cuppa in before tea break.

I had some good fun with Marky Mark over the years, he was a generation younger than me, but we shared the same sense of humour. We had a water fight one day that left us both dripping and the toilet in hell of a mess. He'd sneaked up to ambush me, but I was a step ahead. It must have been shut down time, I think I'd given him a dowsing earlier in the day. He was working on a big wash machine. He was wary of an attack so put his best man outside the machine to keep an eye. Glen Osbourne, AKA Chewbacca.

Now Glen is a big man, must be six feet four, and thickset. Sorry Glen, but you do have a slight resemblance to Chewbacca. Anyway, Glen was meant to be keeping a lookout, but I was teamed up with Steve Battle. They didn't stand a chance. Glen was as good as the lookout on the Titanic as Steve crept in close and gave Glen the eyeshot. This was our favourite target, as it temporary blinded the opposition and gave you time to get yourself out of there. So, Steve hit Glen and he was staggering around like a headless chicken. Poor Mark, he had nowhere to run. I gave him a good soaking.

Of course, I knew Mark well enough to know he'd want revenge.

So, it was with that in mind that I hid an extinguisher in the toilet in case he came after me at going home time.

Sure enough, as I'm washing up he bursts through the door like Rambo. I run to a cubicle and grab my weapon, anybody left in the toilet scarpered and we went full pelt at each other. I don't know how much of that rank water I swallowed that day, but my god, it gave me the "Rodney Trotters," for about three days. Once we had emptied the water over each other, we had to clear up the mess. I must have been nearly forty then, so mature!

An incident whilst the water period was on brought about the discovery of a pervert amongst our midst. Not sure why the lads would want to throw water at me while I was in the shower? But I'm glad they did this particular day. I was happily showering away unaware of the drama that was unfolding. I can't remember all the names who came up to the showers that day. Marky Mark, Steve Beavis and Brian Crease for sure, man mountain Gordon Beattie was with them I'm sure. I say that because he was a notorious water chucker. I have to say, they were a bit amateurish because they arrived at the scene without a bucket between them. Looking around, they opened the door which was the service door that ran behind the shower cubicles. Like a rabbit caught in the headlights was a fitter out of one of the maintenance departments (Not ours, thank god) squatted down watching me shower through a spy hole. I can say with confidence he was watching me as I was the only one taking a shower.
'Trev come out quick.' Like I was going to fall for that one.

‘Only you Muppets would come up here and want to throw water at me while I’m naked in the shower.’ I could tell by the excitement in their voices that something had happened. So, I show my face, still half expecting a bucket of water when they told me they had just seen this guy checking me out. Now, even I found this hard to believe, although I always say I’m a highly tuned athlete, I must have been mid to late-thirties when this happened, and was fondly named by Gordon, a name he still calls me to this day, "The Big Fella." A polite way of calling me fat.
‘Who was it?’ I demand to know.
‘Don’t know his name, but he works out of the P13 crib.’ Revealed, Steve.
‘Right.’ P13 was close to the shower room, so I donned my jeans and shoes and marched down to the said crib like “Tarzan.” A few guys were still milling around. Seeing me arrive without a shirt on drew their attention.
‘Which one of you has just been caught wanking at me from behind the shower cubicle?’ I demanded an answer.
Not an everyday question to ask, I’ll grant you.
‘Not me, Trev.’ When I think back to that day it was quite funny, all these guys protesting their innocence. Mark Christmas, who later became a friend sought me out the next day and revealed who the guy was. What could I do about it? Nothing. Had I beaten the living daylights out of him I would have got myself sacked. So, I let it go. Occasionally I’d see the pervert in question, but he’d scurry along avoiding eye contact.

Mark and I had our revenge on Tony Lynch a few weeks later. He took us around on the buggy barking out orders for jobs to be done the next day. I was sat on the front with Tony and Marky Mark sat behind.
'I want that painted, get rid of that, sort that mess out, find a home for that. Remember Marky, paint those lines again.' Tony was pointing out things that needed doing as he was driving us around the factory. Perhaps I should have mentioned that Mark and jumped off the buggy as we went past the canteen because Tony was still barking out his instructions.
'Look at the state of that, you sort that out in the morning, Marky.' Eventually, Tony pulled up outside his office and went to jump off.
'Now, yer understand what you've got to do, Marky?' Tony turned around to talk to Mark, only to find he had gone. He jumped up and pointed to me.
'Where's that kunt gone?'
'Not sure, Tony. I think he jumped off outside the canteen.'
This was all too much for our Tony, he went into meltdown with me.
'Yer stupid kunt. Why didn't you say he'd jumped off? I've been talking to him for the past ten minutes!'
'Not strictly true, Tony. You thought you were talking to him for the last ten minutes.'
'No one likes a clever kunt.' With that, he went into his office and slammed the door. A little while later Mark came strolling back. I thought it better to tip him off.

'Put your earplugs in, Lynchy is just about to perm your ears.'

Tony had a dislike to the convenor, the *rat*. He thought he was a crook, something I was beginning to wonder myself. It was the time of the grand opening of the gym. The carpet had just been laid, and the carpet fitters were on their way out of the plant. Tony phones me all excited.
'Get your arse over to the office, now.' Thinking one of the lads had got themselves into a pickle, I hurried over.
'Where the fuck have you been?' Tony was waiting for me outside the office.
'Last time I looked, I was Trevor Whitehead, not Linford Christie.' He threw a set of car keys at me.
'Come on, I want you to follow the van.'
'Follow the van? What van?'
'The van that's just laid the carpet in the gym. I've heard it's on its way to Benfleet to fit a new carpet to the convenors new house.'
'Who told you that?'
'Never you mind that, just drive you kunt.'
The reason I asked was I had recently done a wind up on the phone on him. This was around the time you could dial a number and a prerecorded message would play a joke on you. I got a number that played a message about a man accusing you of sleeping with his wife.
One late shift I watched Tony go off to the toilet. So, I put a note on his desk and wrote, "Ring this number urgently."

I hovered about and watched him walk back into the office. I waited until I could see him reading the note then pick the phone up. As I walked into the office I did my best not to laugh.
'Wah ... Hang on a minute. I don't know your wife, listen, mate, you've got the wrong man.' Tony slammed the receiver down.
'Who was that, the wife?'
'Wha? No, some kunt has given my name out to some idiot.' He never knew he's been talking to a message.
I get in the car and Tony jumps in beside me.
'Come on, follow the van.' He barks at me again.
'Isn't the point of following the van to have the van in sight?'
'Don't you worry about that, I know where the convenors new house is.' So, I drive us to Benfleet. It was that journey that I discovered Tony would have made a fantastic driving instructor.
'Speed up yer Kunt, next right, right yer kunt.'
'It's one way, I can't turn right.'
'I know that I mean next right after this one. Slow down, it's around here somewhere?'
'I thought you knew the house?'
'I know the road, it's on this road for sure.'
'Well that narrows it down, can only be around two hundred houses on this road!'
I drive up and down slowly until Tony shouts at me.
'Stop, it's that one.'
'What, the one without the van?'
'Well, it took you so long to get here, they must have fitted the carpet and fucked off.'

'Or they fitted the carpet before they came and fitted the gym out.'
'Of course, that's what they did.'
So, we sat in the little Lancia, pondering our next move. Or Tony sat and pondered my next move.
'Go and check through the window.' Now this alleged house was, in fact, a bungalow. The road was quite hilly, so the front bay window looked quite high.
'How fucking tall do you think I am, Tony?'
'Don't be a kunt. Look, there's a ladder leaning against the side wall.' Sure enough, an old wooden ladder was laying on its side. So, Joe Muggings gets out to check if a new carpet had been fitted. I walk over and pick the ladder up and manoeuvre it up to the front window, which was a good seven feet high. Happy I have the ladder steady, I then climb up and peer through the window. It was at this point I found out that my dear Irish foreman had made a huge mistake. For as I peered through the window I could see a very old white-haired lady staring back at me. I can still hear the screams now. I think it's safe to say that has been my quickest ladder decent in thirty plus years as a Hoist man. I ran to the car, started it and accelerated away.
'Wrong house?' Asked Tony.
'What made you think that?'
'The screaming.'
Tony decided to stop for a beer on the way back. With the aid of a Guinness or two, he soon shifted the blame to me.
'Had yer not been so slow coming to the office, we could have followed the van.'

Now unbeknown to me at the time, this bungalow, not the one with the old woman I frightened in, but the one the *rat* had purchased would lead to the undoing of his reign. That story will come later.

As I write this I guess work wise this was my happiest time. We had a good little team and we met up socially occasionally. The banter and the jokes made the working day just a bit easier.
Gordon Beattie vs Mark Lewin (Bones) You couldn't get a bigger miss-match. It would be like Mike Tyson taking on a featherweight. But I'm not talking fisticuffs here, I'm talking eating a sausage roll. Each morning we'd put our order in for rolls and one of the lads would pop outside the gate to a converted caravan where Mary would sell her rolls. Now I'm talking bread rolls here, stuffed with a sausage. She must have made a small fortune as one week developed.
Now to be fair to Bones, he could eat for a little un. Regularly he would tuck three or four away in the morning tea break. Not bad for a guy who was about seven stone wet through. Gordon was getting the rolls this week and if Bones ordered three, he'd have four. Next day, he ordered four, so Gordon had five. 'Christ Bones, where do you put it?' I asked. I knew where Gordon put it because he looked like the Michelin man.
'I burn it off, Big Fella.'
You can't eat as many as me, Bones.' Gordon threw out the challenge.

'Right, get me six tomorrow.'
'You can't eat six.' Responded Gordon.
'You'll see.' Well, the next morning's tea break couldn't come around quick enough. Gordon set off to Mary's with a mega order of rolls. He had to get a bigger box.
We sit in anticipation as Gordon returns with this big box of rolls. Eventually, six are placed in front of Bones, and Gordon put six in front of himself. The rest of us mere mortals tucked into our one or two rolls.
Thinking back, I remember Bones polishing off four quite quickly. Roll five you could see was a struggle, roll six became a bit of a mountain to climb. Gordon just munched his way through five with ease, but roll six looked more of a struggle.
'If you match me, Bones, I'll concede. As you are a lightweight. So, the two of them attacked roll six and with a real struggle Bones managed to get it down, helped with the odd slurp of tea. As he swallowed the last mouthful, he stood and raised an arm in victory.
'What you doing, Bones?' Asked a smiling, Gordon.
'I matched you, so I'm the winner.'
'Not so fast.' Gordon stood up, went outside and returned with another sausage roll. He'd hidden one up just in case. Gordon sat there eating it as Bones had a deflated look on his face.
Didn't see much of Bones the rest of the day, I think the overeating had caught up with him and he spent the majority of the day in the toilet.
Next day? Normal service was resumed.

It's only been recently that I've managed to catch up with Gordon. He left the plant soon after the sausage roll challenge and moved up Lincoln way. I hadn't spoken to him for well over twenty-five years. But one day on my Facebook his name appeared on people I might know. We became friends and then had some video chats. My god, we laughed a lot about those years we worked together.

So, happy times at work, and soon I was in for some fun with Pat von Brown.

Chapter 7

The Elstree experiences.

Things started to change at work, and not for the better. I must admit it was around this time I started to get my doubts about the convenor. He was agreeing with some strange ideas and without any resistance. I don't think I was alone in this train of thought. So, when the company wanted to implement an operation called MBU, we told the *rat* no way. It was obviously the new flavour of the month. Manufacturing business units to give it its full title. To the laymen out there it basically meant splitting the factory up into different units. I didn't understand the logic then, and I don't understand the logic now.

So, they needed the trade union support to implement it, we didn't like it. In a bid to try and win us over, they decided to take us to a hotel for five days, and give us a seminar of how this would work in our factory. Obviously thinking a bit of wining and dining would do the trick? They put us up in a very plush hotel in Elstree. Now, the first thing that made me laugh was the hotel were a tad short on rooms. Luckily, I arrived early and was given a very nice room. My next-door neighbour, the village idiot, Pat Von Brown. The *rat* arrived late, he'd been to some freebie day out somewhere. I happened to be in the foyer when he arrived

'***** ***, checking in.'

'I'm sorry Mr ***, we have a shortage of rooms, were just making one available in the basement.'
'Basement?' The *rat* tried the do you know who I am, but they didn't budge. So, he was not best pleased. While I was stood there, the actress who played Bianca in Eastenders walked past. Patsy Palmer, you couldn't miss her. Bright orange hair and freckles. I couldn't think of her real name so I tried another tactic to get her attention.
'Ricky,' I shouted out, giving it my best impression. She turned around and looked at me. Then gave me the single finger.
Not what I hoped for, but not the last time I would see her. It wasn't until later, after a few more "EastEnders" characters were spotted that I realised the hotel was dead opposite the Elstree film studios. Some of the cast came across and used the swimming pool and gym.

It didn't take me long to have some fun with Pat. I mentioned to him the first evening that I was going to have a swim and a sauna before breakfast.
'That sounds like a good idea, give me a knock can you, Trev?'
So, at six am the following morning, I knock on Pat's door. Now I think I mentioned earlier that Pat looked like he was ready to rob a bank. He had one of those rubbery face looks, he'd fit into a sketch on "Spitting Image," no problem. Now, this hotel ran a couple of film and an adult viewing channel. It wasn't cheap, I think it was around seventeen pounds per twenty-four hours. To subscribe all you had to do was punch

your room number and the hash key on your phone and you were subscribed. So, this first morning, after the shock of seeing Pat's straight out of bed look, which not only consisted of his rubber face, slit eyes but the most hideous paisley pyjamas I'd ever seen.
'Come on then, Pat. Shake a leg.'
'Hang on a minute, I need a pee.' He went into the bathroom and I quickly walked over to his phone, I picked up the receiver and tapped in the necessary numbers and our Pat was "Porned up."
I decided not to mention the porn channel until later in the day, I didn't want the others knowing .... Not yet.
So, we head off to the fitness centre, and very nice it was too. They gave us a towel and we got changed and took a quick shower.
'Let's have a swim first Pat, then we'll finish with a sauna.' I suggested.
After a few lengths, Pat climbed out and went into the sauna. I soon followed and Pat was sitting in there naked and stone cold.
'What's this meant to do, Trev? I don't feel any different?'
'Well Pat, it would help if you switched the heater on.' I stepped outside and flipped the switch.
'Give it a couple of minutes and let the heater warm up, Pat.'
Now, obviously, this was Pat's first sauna experience.
'I always thought they'd be a log fire in here, Trev.'
'Don't be a clown, Pat. Who's going to look after a log fire in the middle of a fitness centre, we're not sitting on a Swiss mountain resort, are we?'

He sat and looked at the heater and wore a worried look on his face.
'But that heater, it's electric, Trev.'
'Nothing a matter with your eyes, is there?' I reached out and could feel the heat rising up. With just my towel around me, I walked outside and filled the wooden bucket up with water. I came back inside and picked up the ladle.
'What are you doing with that, Trev?'
How do you think a sauna works, Pat? You throw water on the heater.
'Are you mad, you can't throw water on electric, you'll electrocute us.' As I went to throw Pat launched himself at me and we both flew out the door, stark naked. We ended up in a big heap on the floor right in front of a couple of female guests who were just about to enter the sauna.

After that bit of embarrassing excitement with Pat, I was ready for a hearty breakfast. However, a drama was unfolding in the dining room as I entered. I could see a couple of staff and a man in a suit talking to the *rat*. Geoff was sitting at a table so I walked over to join him.
'We could be going home, Trev.'
'Why, what's happened?' Now I immediately thought the rat had at last grown some balls and told the management to stick their MBU's where the sun doesn't shine.
Alas, it was something far more important. The kitchen had run out of eggs.

'How can I have a cooked breakfast with no eggs?' I could hear the *rat* moaning.
'You stick me in a broom cupboard of a room, now this. What kind of hotel are you running here?'
I think *the* rat made such a fuss, they sent somebody out to get some eggs from a local shop. I was so glad to see our convenor focused on the important issues that lie ahead.
Of course, it didn't take long for Pat to make a fool of himself. You have to remember we're dining with the hierarchy of the company. A certain dress code had to be followed. So, when Pat strolled in for his breakfast in his carpet slippers, it was all getting too much for poor, *rat*.
'Pat, for fuck sake, we're not on holiday here.' Pat scurried off to put on the correct attire.

Something Alan Phillips and myself quickly noticed about Pat, he ate as if somebody was about to take his plate away, and if a drink was put in front of him, he'd drink it. The latter we tested later that morning. Pat was sat around a table between Alan and me. Various "Experts," were trying to sell the MBU idea to us. Of course, little did we know the *rat* was most probably already on board and we were just being wined and dined to soften the blow. As another speaker started I filled up our glasses with fresh orange juice out of a pitcher. Pat straight away downed the whole glass. Alan and I looked at each other and winked. Alan filled Pat's glass up again and within seconds he couldn't resist, so he knocked it

back. These were half pint glasses, so he had already downed a pint.
'No more,' he protested as I went to fill it up a third time.
'Who do you think that is?' Asked Alan to distract Pat. While he was turned I filled him up again.
Of course, he couldn't help himself and within a minute he was drinking again, albeit at a slower pace.
'Isn't that one of the girls from EastEnders?' I point across to the fitness centre which was in view from our conference room. Quick as a flash, Alan not only filled Pat up but changed our pitcher for a new full one.
'No, I don't recognise her, Trev.' Pat turned back and immediately started drinking again. Within a minute he'd knocked it back. He now had two pints of fresh orange juice in him. He was overloading on vitamin C. This went on until Alan made the mistake of filling Pat's glass to the rim.
'No more, Alan.' Protested Pat.
Of course, it was only a matter of time before temptation got the better of him. However, because the glass was so full Pat had to stand up, lean forward and slurp it up. I can only describe the noise as similar to a horse. It was so loud that everything stopped and everybody looked around to see Pat making a fool of himself. Poor *rat,* he stuttered and gave Pat one of his disapproving looks.
If that wasn't bad enough for Pat, he now was suffering from orange juice overload. It caused the same effect as five pints of beer. He went out to relieve himself, then found he had to go every fifteen

minutes. Not helped by Alan's top-ups, Pat was up and down like a fiddler's elbow. Every time he got up it disrupted the meeting. By lunchtime, the *rat* had seen and heard enough and gave Pat a right roasting.
'What's up with you, Pat? I heard you made a fool of yourself in the sauna this morning? Exposing yourself to two women. Turn up for breakfast in your slippers, then constantly disrupting the meeting?'
'It's not my fault. Trevor tried to electrocute me and Alan keeps filling my glass up!'
The *rat* looked at Pat and did a fair impression of Captain Mainwaring.
'You stupid boy.'

That evening over dinner, Pat tapped me up about his adult channel.
'Here, Trev. Have you got porn on your TV?'
'No, Pat. You have to pay for it.'
'Really? Well, I've got it.'
'Well, I wouldn't mention it. You're not in the convenors good books at the moment. The last thing he needs is a bill for your porn.'
'Good thinking. Mind you I've not ordered it, must be left on there from the previous person.'
'Yes, that will be it, Pat.'

Next morning, I did the same routine. Knocked Pat up, then while he was in the bathroom, I ordered another 24 hours of porn for Pat's room. This time he didn't play up in the sauna as the two women we'd exposed ourselves too were already in there and throwing water on the heater. I was just getting out

of the swimming pool when I saw the two women rush out of the door. I took a shower, took my shorts off and wrapped a towel around me and joined Pat.
'I thought I was in there for a minute.' He informed me.
'But as soon as I hung my towel up, they scarpered?' Bless Pat, he didn't have a clue about sauna etiquette.
'I'm not surprised, you should keep your towel on.'
'I watched a film last night, and they were all sitting in this sauna, naked!'
'What film?'
'I don't know what it was called. It was on the porn channel.'

The next morning I'd overslept. The time I knocked for Pat, he'd already gone down. Deciding to give a swim and sauna a miss, I went back to my room, got changed and went off for breakfast. I waited for lift and eventually, it arrived and took me to the ground floor. As the doors slipped open, I was faced with Pat, standing in his brief speedos, no towel and dripping wet.
'What's with the "Tarzan" look, Pat?'
'I forgot my towel and clothes, Trev.' Only Pat could do something like that, and the way Pat's luck was running, it was no surprise that the convenor walked past with one of the managers on their way to breakfast. Looking at Pat he nodded his head in dismay.

I had to be a bit sneaky at lunchtime and slip Pat's key in my pocket. I quickly went up to his room and ordered more porn on his behalf. On my way back, I did something I'm not proud of. I was in need of a poo. So, shot into the toilets next to the reception. As I entered a cubicle I could see a room key on the floor. I looked at the key fob number and smiled when I recognised whose room it belonged to. So, I had a poo. Didn't flush, nipped into the cubical next door to clean up. Then on my way out, I dropped the key neatly on top of the pile of shit.

Walking back into the dining room I saw the key holder.

'****, I'm not sure, but I think you dropped your key in the toilet.'

The *rat* searched his pocket.

'You could have picked it up.' He stood up and walked off.

Five minutes later he walked back in and gave me a disapproving nod. I didn't like to ask him how he fished it out!

That evening I decided to bring the adult viewing to a head. The novelty of getting hammered every night had worn thin, so after dinner, I only had a couple of beers and headed to my room. I could hear Pat's TV on. Time for a phone call. In my best Scottish voice, I called his number. The conversation went something like this:

'Am I speaking to Von Brawn?'

'Pat Brown.'
'Ah, sorry Pat von Brawn.'
'No, there's no von in my name. It's just Pat Brown.'
'Sorry, Mr Brawn.'
'How can I help you?'
'Ah … I'm glad you asked that Mr Brawn, it's a bit of a delicate subject.'
'I see, if it's about the sauna, I can only apologise, I thought it was normal behaviour.'
'What did you do in the sauna, Mr Brawn? I hope you weren't masturbating?'
'What … No no, I hung my towel up, that's all. I think I upset a couple of ladies.'
'Don't go worrying about that Mr Brawn, we encourage guests to get naked in the sauna.'
'You do? Oh well, that's okay then.'
'Tell me, Mr Brawn, what time do you normally have a sauna, only I might join you in the morning.'
'Oh …. I think I have an early meeting tomorrow, so may have to give it a miss.'
'That's a shame, Mr Brawn, I could have rubbed some oils in you.'
'Err … Yes, that is a shame. Anyway, if that's all ….'
'What am I like, Mr Brawn, thinking of you, sitting naked in the sauna, sweat dripping off you like droplets of rain …. Oh, it's taken me right off the reason I've called you.'
'Which is?' Asked an embarrassed, Pat.
'The outstanding total of your adult viewing.'
'Oh, I thought it was free.'
'I'm afraid there's no such thing as a free lunch Mr Brawn.'

'But I haven't ordered it, It was already on my television.'
'Mr Brawn, as if I haven't heard that excuse before, it was already on my television.'
'What I meant was, I've not watched any of the films.'
Now-now Mr Brawn. You've watched all the films over the past three days. You see it comes up on our computer who watches what. The only film you haven't watched is a very good homosexual film called "Backdoor Bandits." I could maybe let you watch that film courtesy of the management?'
'No thank you.'
'Now Mr Brawn, I've had the Human resources manager here. He's keeping tabs on the running costs of this seminar. He told me he has no problem paying for all food and drinks, in fact, everything except the adult viewing channel. Now when I told him there was only one of his party using that facility he demanded to know who it was. He said he would tell a Mr Convenor and demand a reprimand. But I told him I have to respect the guest's privacy unless of course, you don't settle your bill.'
'I see, and what is my current bill?'
'Now, let me take a look. It currently stands at fifty pounds, ninety-seven pence.'
'How much?' Pat croaked at me.
'Well three nights at sixteen pounds, ninety-nine pence comes to fifty pounds, ninety-seven pence. Now, Mr Brawn, I'm afraid I need you to come down to reception immediately and clear this bill, otherwise, I'll have to turn off your adult viewing channel.'

Now Pat's response wasn't what I expected.
'Err, can you leave it on for five more minutes?' It took all my willpower not to burst out laughing and give the game away. I took a deep breath and composed myself.
'Okay, Mr Brawn, I'll give you five more minutes. After all, we all have needs, don't we? But I expect you down here in reception shortly to pay your bill.' I hung up and waited.
Now, Pat had a habit of whistling as he walked. So, I soon heard his door close and him whistling away to himself.
Ten minutes later he was back. Oh, I would have loved to be at the reception when he arrived to pay his porn bill.
Next morning, I gave him a knock and when he opened the door he accused me.
'I knew that was you on the phone last night.'
'What you on about, Pat?'
'I knew it was you.' He repeated.
'If you knew it was me, why did you go to reception and make a c*** of yourself.'
'See, I knew it was you, how would you know I went to the reception last night if it wasn't you?'
'Because the convenor has just rung me and told me about the embarrassment you caused at the reception last night.'
'Shit. Do you think he'll send me home?'
'Possible Pat. I'd get a quick sauna and breakfast in before he does.'

I know some of you will read about Pat and have some sympathy for him.
He, despite his stupidity, was a likeable character. I recalled those stories with a smile and fondness.
He should never have been a Shop Steward, let alone a JWC committee member. I did often wonder if his department voted him in as a joke.

The last I heard of Pat he was stranded in Leicester. He'd moved there to be near his daughter. Then she moved away? Make your own mind up about that.

The outcome of the Elstree week, MBU's were agreed and introduced.
If I thought that was bad enough, it was just a preliminary of what was to come my way, something that forced me to quit my role as a union representative.

Chapter 8

Opening a can of worms!

Major changes were coming to the plant. Our company were no longer interested in making our type of vehicle. Now, to us on the factory floor, not only was it a surprise announcement, we just couldn't understand why? We were making a quality product, in the top two of sales. We had built up a great reputation and our product was known worldwide. Enter the Italians.

We soon found out that we were now part of a massive company. But of course, unlike the UK companies, the Italians like to look after their own. Hence, after a honeymoon period, it was announced that at some point in the future, they would be closing the manufacturing side of the engines. Not only would we be losing half our workforce, it made the whole plant vulnerable because the future for our Plant was assembly only. We would become what's known as a screwdriver plant. This at the at the time made for a bleak outlook, the engines would be made in Italy, then shipped to the UK?

The bottom line of all this is our previous company didn't want us. The Italians did. They stepped in and turned the place around. It's testament to their way of running the business that it still thrives today.

The other bad news was we had lost our strength of being part of a big combine of manufacturing factories in the UK. We were now on our own. In time, this would give opportunities of gain to a certain person or persons of influence.

It all started with the nuts and bolts, literally. The company wanted to outsource the small department that delivered the nut and bolt stock to the assembly areas.

I can't remember how many people we were talking about, most probably less than five. They came under the store's umbrella, so Paul Norris was their shop steward. I was their JWC member. Paul and I had a meeting as soon as this rumour surfaced. Up to this point, we'd never allowed contractors to do anything that was classed as in-house work.

The only contractors I knew at that point were the canteen staff and a little cowboy unit that did steel work for hoists. The occasional firm would come in to do work outside the skill set of the maintenance department. Apart from that everything was in-house. Paul and I were adamant, no way could we allow this. To be honest I think the majority of the stewards supported us.

It wasn't just about the nuts and bolts, it was the principle of letting contractors in to take work away from our members.

You would have thought it was a no-brainer, allow it once, and as this chapter heading said, we're opening a can of worms.

Problem was, behind the scenes the *rat* must have agreed on it. He talked some people around and it happened. Now, I could make a statement here about the *rat*, but I think you know my feelings about

him by now. I'll leave it to you to make their own mind up.
Even though Paul and I were so bitterly against it, we got shafted.
Who knows what pressure was applied to the *rat* of a convenor, or what incentive was handed out to him, after all, this is only my slant on what happened. But against all our trade union principles, we allowed in-house work to be put out to contract.
Saying the guys involved would be given work elsewhere in the factory, I'm afraid was a nothing gesture to what was allowed to happen.
Of course, the history of the plant will tell you the future fears of Paul and myself soon came to fruition.

At the time, I didn't know any better. It wasn't until years later when I was on my unions Motor vehicle executive committee. That I met up with maybe fifteen members from places like Nissan, BMW, Ford's, Toyota, Vauxhall and LDV vans, spread all around the country. The majority of these guys were convenors, or Senior Stewards as they liked to be known. It was after talking and building up a network of contact with these guys that I discovered a real flaw in our shop steward set up.
I found out that all of these guys were elected via the factory members. They couldn't believe the system we used.
When you think back, had the *rat*, or any other convenor for that matter. Had to face the shop floor for re-election, do you think he would have been so

easily persuaded to farm work out? I know the answer.
No, it was left to Paul and myself to get it in the neck from the guys on the shop floor.

It wasn't long after that stab in the back, that my favourite band of brothers were under scrutiny. Security and fireman.
After a rocky start, and the problem with the milk put to bed, things had started to settle down. Obviously, there wasn't a lot of love lost between me and Jim McClure and his sidekick George. We'd have a monthly meeting and deal with any problems without any shouting.
The guys themselves seemed to be happy with me, I did still get the occasional letter in the internal post from them, but I would write on the back of the envelope, "Not known at this address, please deliver to security for fingerprint analysis." And send it back.

Now, for some reason, I didn't hear the security and fireman were under threat from our convenor. No, it was a frantic phone call from Jim McClure.
Could I go and see him at my earliest convenience, please?
I'd never heard Jim use such a word. Although our meetings were more civil these days, they weren't friendly.
Add to this, Jim ordering George to make me a cup of tea when I walked into their office, I knew the alarm bells were ringing.
'What's up, Jim?'

'Have you heard? You must have heard? Is it true?'
'I'm not sure what you're talking about, Jim?'
'Contractors, they are looking to contract us out!'
'Really?'
'Yes, you must know something. Now come on Trevor, I know we haven't always been on the best of terms, but you need to be honest with me.'
Trying not to sound like Manuel out of Fawlty Towers I replied.
'I know nothing.'
Jim sat there, face bright red, his blood pressure sky high.
'Calm down, Jim. It's most probably just a rumour. I'll go and have a chat with the convenor and put this to bed.'
'I'm fifty-six, Trev. Where am I going to get another job at my age?'
'You only fifty-six, Jim? I thought you were older than that. Leave this with me and I'll come back and see you.'
I strolled over to the convenors office. To be honest, as much as I was angry about the nuts and bolts, not in my wildest dreams did I think security was under threat. The *rat* was sitting at his desk with his number two, Alan Phillips hovering. I only had to look at the convenors face to know what was coming.
'Alright, I've just had a conversation with Jim McClure. He seems to think the Security and firemen are under threat?'
The *rat* reclined in his chair lit a cigarette and looked at me.
'Yes, they are being looked at.'

‘And you didn’t think to inform me, I have to find out from the guys themselves?’
‘Well, I knew you’d play up.’
‘Play up you c***.’
‘See, that’s no way to talk to your convenor.’
‘You’re a fucking joke. Grow some balls.’ I stormed out and had to break the news to Jim. Who looked almost suicidal on hearing the news.

I think it is safe to say things between the convenor and me were fractious, to say the least. But like the nuts and bolts scenario, behind the scenes, I believe the *rat* had already agreed on the principle. I can’t prove it, I can only write what I thought at the time. A few weeks later, I’m informed that a working party is going to look at some contract security firms in action. I was on a working party, along with Geoff, the *rat* and Alan. Jim was invited along with someone from the H/R and the manager, Monotonous Michael Law.
Perhaps I’m being a bit cruel to Michael, he did think he was the business. I can remember at the *rat’s* wedding, a bit of a lavish do with a live group at the reception. Michael got up and sung with the group, followed by a reluctant me. Now I can’t sing, I’m the first to admit that. However, with Alan Philips seeing a wind-up opportunity, he encouraged me to get up there and represent the hourly paid. That and the aid of about six pints I climb up and killed the “Green green grass of home.”
It’s safe to say I bombed.

We had three firms that had put in a tender to visit. They decided to leave the joke firm until last. The first was a company who looked after a large factory. All very proficient and professional. The second trip we were taken to the BBC studios at the television centre, White City. Again, a firm that was very proficient and they threw in a free lunch at the studios where I spent most of my time celeb spotting and once again seeing my favourite ginger walk past. This time I just smiled and resisted the “Ricky” impersonation. I didn’t get the finger this time, more of an “I’ve trod in dog shit” look.

The last trip was to the Circus Tavern. We met up with a guy who I did wonder years later if Peter Kay had based his character, club owner Brian Potter on. Apart from the bleached blonde hair and minus the wheelchair, he could have been a dead ringer. When you think about how absurd this was. They wanted to use a firm that only security experience was to throw out drunks in a nightclub.
Well, it was obvious who got the contract after I have given you the three firms who had put a tender in. Yes, the factory was now going to be guarded by bouncers!
The guy whose previous job was to look after the entertainer Michael Barrymore, was now looking after a huge factory with millions of pounds worth of assets?
I’m not sure what I can add to this. Two professional security firms had been overlooked. I didn’t like the thought of outsourcing to begin with, and now I had

to face up to these security guys and try and pretend it was the best deal the trade union could get for them?
You see, what was decided, we were obliged to support. It's the trade union way. You may well hate the deal, but you have to show a united front.

I will choose my words carefully. You do have to wonder if certain incentives were exchanged for such a deal!
For me, well I had grown sick of the *rat's* antics. He wasn't answerable to anybody. He'd come out with bullshit to try and convince you it was the best deal. 'It's better to have a company you know, Trevor.' This was his way of explaining his latest deal. It was farcical, and I wondered who else was in on it. Michael Law? Well, maybe he was bemused as me. I never asked him.
I couldn't look the security in the eye. As much as they had been a pain in the arse, the majority of them were decent guys and they were just about to be shafted. Fair play to the likes of Paul Norris and Geoffrey Martin Smith, they stuck it out. For me, I didn't want to be associated with the likes of the *rat* anymore. I resigned and happily got on with my life.

Chapter 9

Outsourced and another comeback.

Over the next few years, I just enjoyed life. I kept myself actively involved with my local Labour Party, and they were exciting times with the launch of New Labour. I'm ashamed to admit at the time I was a fan and worked hard to get Tony Blair elected. He was charismatic and just what we needed to end the Tories long run in power. I'll continue my Labour Party activities later in the book. I was sorry to see some of my old work colleagues leave. Gordon Beattie headed Lincoln way, Bob Fellows decided it was time to try his luck working for himself. The new company were ending the honeymoon period and starting to reduce the workforce. A lot of staff were trimmed as were the hourly paid. Some of my colleagues were shipped out onto production jobs. Life in the plant was changing.

All was going well until a rumour started about the maintenance personnel, we were being looked at as a possible outsourcing target.

At first, I thought that the *rat* was behind another dodgy deal, but as time went past, the name (I won't use the real name) Italian2, came into the frame. We were told that Italian2 was a company that specialised in maintenance type work. Apparently, they were beginning to get into other European Italian owned plants.

So, as we were fast approaching the millennium, I was now working for Italy2.

The one saving factor was that because the Italians owned Italy2, we were staying in the company pension scheme. Unlike the poor security guards.

Now I don't want to be cruel to a couple of guys here. Eddie Priestaff and Richard Llewellyn. Both very nice guys and Richard I knew extremely well via our Labour Party activities. Richard was well liked and respected locally and was a councillor for a number of years. Richard passed away only a few months prior to me writing this book. Eddie passed away a few years back, I heard through the grapevine he'd contracted asbestosis.

You see the problem I soon discovered when we were moved to Italy2 was we were left with, in my opinion, three very weak shop stewards. Like I say, Eddie and Richard were nice guys but weren't militant enough. They'd been around when I was last a steward and I knew them so well. The third person was the infamous Hoof."

I used to say I could write a book about the hoof, and here I am. A more despicable, tight, unethical human being I've yet to meet. A man with absolutely no morals. Sounds like I'm being a tad harsh. Well, see how you feel at the end of this chapter.

So, I had a dilemma, I vowed that I'd never stand for shop steward again. I'd been badly let down by the *rat*. I think the security still held a grudge, as far as they were concerned I was in on them being taken over by a firm of what they described to me as a cowboy unit.

It was only a few months into the Italan2 time when the shop steward elections were due. Now, this was causing me a real dilemma. I was a Transport and General union man. I signed for them when I first started, recommended by my dad. As I mentioned, my dad was a bit of a rebel, so instead of joining the then AEEU, like 95% of his colleagues, he joined the opposition. Now at the time of my two stints as steward, we had plenty of T&G members in the maintenance, so it wasn't a problem for me. But a lot of these guys had left or been moved out of maintenance. Knowing how fickle some of these guys were, I knew it would go against me in an election. Also, something the hoof would use to try and take votes away from me. So, I changed unions. I can remember being called over to see the *rat* who amongst other things was my branch secretary with the T&G.

I walked in and he tried to play to the audience.

'Oh, here he is, not good enough for you now? I'm disappointed with you, Trevor.'

'Well, I know how that feels, I've been disappointed with you for years, you C***.'

A briefest of meetings.

I sat back for a while until a few of the guys approached me. Like me, they were worried, especially now as the hoof was apparently the self-elected senior steward. So, I threw my name in, and the hoof, being the snake, he was, said I would be going up against Richard. I thought it would be a general vote and pick the top three. He changed that because he knew he would be shipped out. So, I faced Richard in the election and received more votes. I felt sorry for Richard because he'd been a long-standing steward.

I hadn't had much to do with the hoof up to that point. He entered union life as I quit. I heard stories about him, none that were complimentary. Geoff told me about an incident with him.
They'd been out so meeting somewhere and decided to stop at a Chinese restaurant on the way home. I can't remember how many of them, not many I know. So, Monotonies Michael Law, the manager goes to pay the bill. Checking his wallet, he realised he'd forgotten the company credit card. Not owning one of his own, he asked if one of the others could pay the bill and he'd settle up with them the next day. Geoff said the hoof flew out of his chair, ran over to the till and asked for a pair of scissors? He then got his credit card out and cut it up? Unbelievable .... But true. I asked him about this incident some years later and he told me the card had run out of date.
'If it had run out, you didn't have to cut it up, the restaurant wouldn't have accepted it.'
'Well ... It had nearly run out.' Bloody tight arse.

So, I knew all about the Hoof. Now for people reading this wondering why he was known as the "Hoof," he suffered from *congenital talipes equinovarus.* Or in layman's terms, he had a club foot. Now, this handicap never stopped him being one of the first out the gate at clocking off time.

Now, one thing in my favour, no one liked the hoof, especially Eddie Priestaff, who was still smarting over the way he changed the election procedure to save himself. So, I went to see Eddie and he soon got behind me as I was about to clip the hoofs mane.

'We should have a meeting, I suggested. Get ourselves organised.' The hoof was a snake, always remember that. He knew what I was after and he tried his best to avoid a meeting, which was ridiculous.
'Well I'm a bit tied up the rest of this week, then I'm on holiday next week.'
'No problem. We'll have one when your back off your holidays.' So, the hoof was happy and when he went on holiday, Eddie and I went to the little office we were given by Italy2 to run our union business and emptied all the hoof's stuff and put it in a cardboard box.
On his return, I went to see him.
'Nice holiday?'
'Yes, great.'
'Good. Now. I've emptied your stuff out of my drawers and put it all in a cardboard box for you. Can you ship it out of the office today, it's in the way.'
'You can't-do that, I'm the senior steward.'

'No, you *were* the senior steward. Unfortunately, Eddie and I don't want you as our senior steward, so Eddie backed me.'
'You can't-do that, I wasn't at the meeting.'
'Well, I've organised a meeting for ten this morning, you can speak about it then.'
Simple. In fact, so simple it's a pity the stewards didn't adopt the same tactics with the *rat*?

At the time, we didn't know how long we'd remain with Italy2. Although I thought we were doing okay under them, I couldn't see it being a permeant arrangement, no money to be made. I Had the usual suspects that were never happy. One, an electrician, Dickie Burton. He used to bend my ears regularly.
'It's not right, Trevor. We should have an H/R person here permanently.'
There were less than one hundred of us and he wanted some poor sod to be in the plant permanently.
'If you have a problem, I can ring and they will send somebody down. Trust me, we don't want H/R here.'
What a cock.

I'd joined the AEEU just at the time it was merging with the staff union the MSF. This merger of unions produced a new name, Amicus. I went along to my local branch meeting; the secretary was a full-time union officer. The hoof had wriggled himself into being the chairman. So, I sat through the business and stopped and had a beer with the officer afterwards. The hoof, not wanting to open his wallet

used to slope off. This continued for about six months until one night he asked me if I'd ever considered being a bit more pro-active?
Well, of course, I did. Within weeks of that approach, I found myself in the role of the new Branch Secretary.
This, of course, put the hoofs nose out.
'I've been coming to this branch for years, I've never been asked?'
'Yes, and for years you've not put your hand in your pocket and bought the secretary a drink.' I soon straightened the hoof out.

This little promotion opened some more doors for me. I received a strange phone call asking me if I was interested in getting a position on the executive committee of the newly formed Amicus union. They wanted me on the eastern region committee.
I was a bit sceptical, but I thought I'd go to this meeting and see what's what. It was held in a pub in Ipswich. I didn't know a sole but introduced myself. Contacts details were swapped along with phone numbers.

A month later I get an invitation letter to go to the first meeting of the Amicus Eastern Region. This meeting was to elect members to the Regional committee.
It was held on a Saturday, again in the Suffolk area. The time I was driving home, I was now a member of the Eastern Region Executive Committee.

Within six months of moving away from the T&G, I was now in the union's hierarchy.
I guess I was in the right place at the right time.

The perk of these added responsibilities was more paid time off from work. Something I don't think the company were overjoyed about but were obliged to release me.

If the sudden change in fortunes caught me off guard, it was nothing compared to the changes that came in my Labour Party activities.
For years I'd been a member of my local party, Basildon & Billericay. I used to go most months to the meetings and during any election period I would step up and help out, albeit delivering leaflets or the dreaded door knocking.
I guess it's fair for me to admit I wasn't overly keen on that task. Especially when you're campaigning in a Tory stronghold. But it had to be done, and I went at it with my normal enthusiasm. That's why I hold Richard Llewellyn is such high regard. He would always hold his own in an argument about politics. He was known as the "Riddler," amongst the shop stewards. He could ramble on about something for an hour, at the end of the conversation you'd forgotten what the question was. But face to face on a doorstep, he was in his element.
Now, I'd heard a whispering about some boundary changes but didn't for the life of me think it would have any effect on me. How wrong was I?

I lived in Wickford, and because of that, I was shipped to the new constituency of Rayleigh & Wickford. The hoof lived in Wickford, but he wasn't so active on the political front as me.
Well, a few months had passed and I hadn't heard anything about this new formation. In the end, I phoned up the Labour Party head office and was informed they'd already had a couple of meetings?
'I haven't been informed of any meetings?' I stated.
To cut a long story short, the girl I spoke to said she would contact the Rayleigh & Wickford CLP secretary and get him to contact me about the next meeting.
Sure enough, through the post came a large envelope with the previous meetings minutes and the time and date of the next meeting.
I read through the minutes and I couldn't believe what was written, it was unbelievable. I'll give you a couple of examples:

"Election of Chairman:
As nobody stood, John ******** Said he would reluctantly carry on.
Election of the secretary:
As nobody was willing to take on this role, David**** Said he would carry on."

I sat and read through the remaining minutes. Nothing about fundraising, guest speakers, advertising. No treasury reports. No treasurer was mentioned. At the bottom was the next meeting. Luckily it was going to be in Wickford. Time for some action. I had to get the hoof active. So, I phoned him

and told him what had happened. He didn't seem too interested until I mentioned the chairman's position.
'Sounds like there crying out for an experienced chairman. Think about it, Chairman of your local Labour Party is a prestigious position.'
'When did you say the meeting was again?' I had him hooked.
I agreed to pick him up, the first time I'd been to his house, and one I'll never forget. It had been raining and the hoof's wife Brenda answered the door.
'He's just getting ready Trevor, come in.' I was wearing a nice pair of Nike trainers, I'd only just got them. But I kicked them off in the hallway and followed Brenda into the lounge. They had one of those ugly dogs, a British Bulldog Terrier. He kept trying to jump up at me. Brenda grabbed him and chucked him in the hallway.
'Sorry about that, he can go up and torment ****.'
She made me a cup of tea and said she would go up and hurry him up.
Five minutes later he came down.
'Right are we fit?'
'Yes, let's go.' I walk out into the hallway and my trainers are no longer there?
Where're my trainers?'
'I don't know, maybe Brenda put them away somewhere.' He opened the under stairs cupboard, but no trainers to be seen. So, he called up the stairs.
'Brenda, have you seen Trevor's trainers?'
I look up and see Brenda coming down all embarrassed carrying the remains of my trainers.

Remains maybe not the right word to describe two rubber soles.
'I'm so sorry, Trevor, the dog has had a go at them, they looked expensive.'
'They were, Brenda.' The hoof takes a look and comes out with a rather stupid statement.
'Leave them here, Brenda can fix them.'
'Well, I'm not sure there is much I can do.'
'Have a go. Borrow a pair of my shoes for now.' He disappeared under the cupboard again and came out with a pair of white trainers.
Now, although they were my size, there was a slight problem. I didn't have a hoof, so the right trainer had been built up. So, when I walked, it looked like I had a limp. Because we were now running late, I had no choice. We trotted out to my car like a couple of thoroughbreds.
Of course, no mention of paying for a new pair of trainers entered the conversation as we drove to the community centre.
As I pulled up, I sensed something was wrong. There wasn't another car in the car park. I could see someone standing by the door.
'That looks like Diana Taylor.' I tell the hoof.
'Wait here.' I got out of my car and hobbled over to her. Now Diana was a very active and outspoken member of the local Labour Party. I'd known her for years. She was another one like the hoof and me who had been moved from the Basildon & Billericay group. Unfortunately, she'd had a heart attack and wasn't in the best of health. She stood there holding her walking stick as I approached.

‘What have you done to your foot, Trevor?’ Not wanting to discuss it I quickly dismissed the question.
‘Just a slight sprain. What’s going on here, Diana?’
‘Those bastards from Rayleigh have moved the meeting back to their place.’
‘They never notified me.’
‘No, they wouldn’t. I’ve just rung their secretary and he said because of the lack of interest from the Wickford members they decided to keep the meetings at Rayleigh.’
‘Did they now. Come on Diana, well track these c**** down and sort it.’
The pair of us headed over to my car. As I’m getting in, the hoof is trying to bundle Diana in the back.
‘Let Diana sit in the front, for fuck sake.’
The hoof, no scruples at all.
‘I drive to Rayleigh like a man possessed, to say I’m pissed off is an understatement. What with my trainers and now these clowns playing silly buggers I was ready for a showdown. Maybe it was my red hair, but once the switch was flicked, that was it. Nothing got held back.
I eventually find the village hall, pull up and the three of us walk in, or I should say limp in. If you’ve watched a three-legged race, double that and you’d get an idea of what we looked like entering the hall that night. I can still see the setting now. Two men at the back of the hall behind a table. One about seventy, bald. He was a double for the little guy Benny Hill used to slap on the top of his head. The other, a man of about sixty. Thick set and heavy-rimmed glasses. Four others were sat, three elderly

women who would have looked more at home in the snug of the "Rovers Return" and another bald man, but this one had a bushy beard. He looked like he had his head on upside down. Our entry had killed any conversation that was taking place at that time. We sat down and the evening's entertainment took only seconds to get underway. The bald man behind the table pointed at me.

'The meeting started thirty minutes ago. Coming in here disrupting us without a bye or leave. Who the hell do you think you are?'

Well, that was the ignition switched flicked. I stood up, walked over and grabbed him by the tie.

'Listen c***. I'm a member from Wickford, if you ever move the meeting venue without notifying me again, I promise you, you'll live to regret it.' Well, you could have heard a pin drop.

'Who are you?' Asked the man wearing the glasses.

'I'm a member of this constituency. Who are you?'

'I'm the secretary.'

'Oh, so you are the pair of clowns who hold these two positions because no one else wanted them. Well, let me tell you something now. You have these positions because you kept the first meeting hush-hush. You never notified any of the Wickford members of the inaugural meeting. Well enjoy your brief reign, because next month we will come mob-handed, we'll put a vote of no confidence up for the pair of you, and trust me when I tell you, you'll be history.'

I went to sit down. The bald man threw the strangest of questions at me.

'Well, where were you in 1953?' I turned and looked at him.'
'I wasn't even born then, cock.'
'Precisely.' I never did find out what he was on about. We sat through the rest of the now subdued meeting until it came to any other business. I shot my hand up then stood up and delivered a damning speech about what had gone on. How did they expect to get new members carrying on the way they did? I won't bore you with the details, let's just say for ten minutes I lashed them. Eventually, they closed the meeting and the chairman and secretary hurried out without a second glance. The three old women came over and you'd have thought the lottery had come up.
'My god, we've been waiting years for those two to be put in their place, well done. You'll get our vote.'
'Well I suggest we put the hoof up for chairman, he has a lot of experience in that role, and we'll try and find a suitable secretary.'
'You need to be the secretary. You are the type of man we want.'
'You'll get my vote, Trevor.' Diana smiled. Oh well, it looked like I had a shot at being the new secretary. I had a month to drum up support and get them to the next meeting.
As I started to contact Wickford members, it all fell easily onto my lap. I received a letter from the current secretary telling me that the chairman and himself were resigning from their roles. Due to ill health, according to the letter.

It was a shame, I didn't go to that meeting to take his job. Just shake the tree a bit. But if I'm honest, the pair of them shouldn't have been holding those types of positions. As far as I was concerned, New Labour was the future. These old dinosaurs had to go.

A few days later at work, the hoof was walking around in sunglasses.

'What's up with you? Is it a tribute to Stevie Wonder night?'

'No, my dogs died.' If he was looking for sympathy, he'd come to the wrong guy.

'Be those trainers of mine he ate, that will teach him. Most probably the glue got stuck in his intestines, was he in much pain when he died?' The hoof hobbled off distraught.

The sorrow didn't last long for he was soon hobbling around with a smile on his face.

'What, you get a refund on the vet's bill?'

'No, we got a new dog, a puppy.'

'What type?'

'Same as the last one.' So, the hoof had put his hand in his pocket for a new dog. A dog that would soon enough leave his mark on me.

I should have known better than to go around his house after seeing him walking around with a black eye.

'Christ, what's happened to you?'

'Well, I went to my daughters for Sunday dinner, she lives at Burnham on Crouch. I thought I'd take the dog for a walk. Well, all was going well, I took him off his lead and he was having a great time. All of a

sudden, he spotted a cat in a garden, and he was away. The bloody dog chased this cat for miles, I was running behind trying to keep him in sight. Eventually, the cat ran up this lamppost. I managed to get the dog on his lead when this man walked over to me and shouted, is that your dog? Yes, he is my dog, why do you ask? Because that's my cat up there shitting himself. With that, this bloke thumped me.'
I couldn't help but laugh, but as the old saying goes, he who laughs first laughs last.

About two weeks later I'd arranged to pick the hoof up for a Labour Party meeting. As per normal, I drove, Mr Tightarse would never volunteer to drive. It was my first visit since the trainer's episode and I should have had more sense. Brenda opened the door and immediately advised me to leave my shoes on.
'He's just getting ready, come on through, Trevor. So, I follow Brenda into the lounge and could hear the dog barking and scratching at the kitchen door.
'I heard you got a new dog.'
'Yes, he's a bit of a handful.' Well, I wasn't on the ball because as she opened the door, this dog flew past her, leapt at me and locked itself onto my forearm. I kid you not, this dog was mad. The hoof appeared and between him and Brenda, they prize the dog off my arm, which now had six puncture holes and blood running out.
'For fuck sake, you pair shouldn't own a fucking dog. The last one wrecked my trainers, which by the way

you owe me seventy quid for, and now you have a dog that draws blood to your guests.' I stormed out.
'What about the meeting, Trev?'
'You go, I'm off to the hospital, the way my luck is with you I've most probably contracted rabies.'
'You don't have to worry about that, he's had all his injections.'
I won't write the reply I gave him. I'll leave that to your imagination.
So, after two visits to the hoofs, I've arrived home once on a wet night in just my socks, and this time with my arm bandaged up and a course of tetanus injections to look forward to.

There was something about the hoof, I guess the best way to sum him up is he was an unsavoury character. One of these people that would invade your private space. You'd talk to him and he'd keep edging nearer. Notorious if a woman was around and had some perverted ways. I can remember Geoff telling me they'd been to London with their wives and while waiting for the train, hoof handed Geoff some of what he thought were business cards. When he looked, they are call girl cards, he'd been picking them up out of the phone boxes.
'Here, put these in your wallet, you never know?'
I never saw his collection of porn, but allegedly he had the biggest collection of porn for a private collector in Essex. He got barred from our "Tug club," early on for so-called losing a film?

Anyway, he was behaving himself as my chairman of the union branch and the local Labour Party.
I thought a miracle had happened one night when we'd gone to a meeting in Chelmsford. It was a union meeting and secretary's and chairman were invited. So, we go and as we walk in I'm called over by a couple of Ford guys from Dunton who I got to know from my involvement in the Eastern Region set up. Les McDonald and John Scarola, a couple of decent guys and good union reps. Hoof disappeared inside and I walk over and have a bit of a networking chat. Well, I looked over and could see the hoof hobbling towards me with two pints in his hands. It was one of those double take moments.
'Here you are Trev, got you a pint.' He gives me the drink then ambles off.
'Fuck me,' I tell the Ford reps.
'I don't know if I should drink this or have it framed. It's the first pint he's bought me.' The bubble didn't take long to burst.
'It's a free bar, Trev.'

After this next incident, I'm going to talk about, by rights, the hoof should have been stood against a wall and shot. He let the trade union down in a big way. He brought shame to our Labour Party constituency and our local branch.
We had to pick a candidate to represent Rayleigh & Wickford at the next General Election. These meetings were called hustings.
Now the timing couldn't have been worse, the meeting date was set at a time I was on holiday.

Now, I put my trust in the hoof, I mean he'd been involved before when we were members of the Basildon & Billericay constituency. What could go wrong?

I reluctantly went to his house a few days before I was due to go away. Only after he promised to have the dog in a cage. Sure enough, when I arrived, the dog was in this large metal cage in the kitchen. When I looked in their lounge, it looked different.

'Had a change round in here?'

'New three-piece suite.'

'Oh, I didn't think you'd had the other one long?'

'Eighteen months. We left the dog in here while we went shopping, came back and he'd eaten and ruined the lot.'

I couldn't help a wry smile.

So, I go through the election procedure, let all the would-be candidates have five minutes to introduce themselves and speak about their vision of representing us at the next election. Then hold a vote.'

'No problem, Trev. You go and have a nice holiday.'

So, I did, I mean, what could go wrong.

I arrive back from holiday and check my answerphone, usual array of messages until one came out that spelt trouble.

'Mr Whitehead, I'm calling from the political office of Amicus the union. I have to say not only me but the general secretary is appalled at your choice of candidate at your hustings meeting for the next General election. We put forward who we thought was the ideal candidate, only to be overturned by one vote in favour of a university graduate. Call me back as soon as you can.'

Now, in my defence, I never knew any of the candidates, I wasn't at the meeting, I'd stupidly left it to the hoof. So, I phone the hoof and tell him to lock the dog up as I'm on my way round. I purposely don't mention the phone message. I arrive and play it cool.
'So, everything go okay at the hustings?'
'Yes, it was a close-run thing between two in the end.'
'Good, have you got copies of their resume?'
'Err …. Somewhere.'
'Find them, I want to see who we have representing us.' Hoof brings his battered briefcase out and hands me a sheet of paper.
'This is who we elected.'
'A woman.'
'Yes, Trev. But what a good speaker.'
'I see. Lives in Nottingham, and knows nothing about our local problems. She must have been a hell of a speaker.'
'She was, Trev.'
'Who was the other person?' Well there was five candidates to start with, then it just came down to these two, this was the other candidate, it was a close run thing I can tell you.' Hoof passed me another sheet of paper, and it soon became clear why I had an angry message left on my answer machine.
'When you say it was a close-run thing, how close?'
'The votes were level, so, I as chairman had the deciding vote.'
'What a surprise, you picked the woman.'

‘But she was a good speaker, Trev.’
‘You’re a stupid C***. You have dropped us right in the shit. I’ve got the hierarchy of the union on my back because of your fucking stupidity.’
‘That’s a bit harsh.’
‘Fucking harsh. Look at this guy’s resume. Twenty years a trade union member, an activist who has loads of experience in the Basildon area. He was put forward by the union, our union, you stupid prick. And you have the deciding vote and don’t pick him, you pick a fucking school girl?
‘But …’
‘If you mention she’s a good speaker again I’ll kick your arse you c***.’ Brenda walked in with all the shouting going on.
‘I’m sorry for the shouting, Brenda. But your husband has done something really stupid.’
‘What have you done?’
‘I picked who I thought was the better speaker.’
‘Well, if I get summoned to head office, you can come with me. Then you can explain why the chairman of our local trade union branch voted against one of our own in favour of a girl.’

In the end, I dealt with the problem. I could have blamed the hoof, but I tried to save face for the branch’s benefit. If you read this hoof, I hope you hold your head in shame. You have the morals of a sewage rat.

Now, there’s a funny ending to this story. I’d like to say justice was served, but the hoof is so thick skinned it just bounced off him. Let me just say the candidate he had chosen got well and truly hammered in the election and was soon on her way back to Nottingham. And trust me when I tell you, she was a crap speaker. But she wore a skirt and that was enough temptation to get the hoofs vote.

Let's jump forward five years. It's heading towards hustings time again. After the last embarrassing disaster, I make sure I am not on holiday. I get an approach at work by Richard Llewellyn. Now Richard knew his politics, he was a councillor and I always had time for him. He asked me how the candidates were shaping up at the forthcoming selection meeting.

I told him I had a couple that looked interesting.

'I have a guy who I'd like you to meet Trev. I think he could do well for you. A local man and a good trade unionist.'

So, we arranged to meet over a beer in a local pub. I ring the hoof and ask if he wants to come and meet a prospective candidate.

The offer of a free beer is just too much for him. So, he says yes.

So as per normal, I drive to the pub, and the four of us meet up. Richard introduces the guy and we get a beer and sit down. Five minutes of general chit chat and then we get down to business. For the life of me, I can't remember the man's name. He was a post office worker, I can remember that.

So, I asked the guy what experience he had.

'Well to be honest Trevor, this is my second attempt. I don't think you were around five years ago when I last stood.'

'I must have been, I've been the Labour Party secretary for seven years now.'
'I don't remember you being at the meeting? I don't know if you remember me then, I was unlucky, I was pipped to the post by the chairman's deciding vote. Some young girl, a university graduate.'
I looked at the hoof who was now starting to perspire and wriggle on his seat.
Oh, deep joy, I wasn't going to let the hoof off this one.
'You mean this c***. He was chairman at that meeting and went against you to pick a school girl.'
The three of us looked at the hoof who avoided eye contact and supped his beer.
'But she was a good speaker.'

The end result to this story was we picked a very good candidate in a guy called Mike Le-Surf, who went on to bigger and better things. I'm still in contact with Mike and can I say what a very good MP he would make. A very good speaker and works extremely hard for the Labour Party.

Chapter 10

Brussels

The hoof was becoming a liability. Well, to be honest, he'd been that all the time I'd known him. Time to ease him out to graze.

I'd known the munch for a number of years. He was quite vocal at meetings and I liked the guy. He knew how slippery the hoof was, and I encouraged him to stand for steward at the forthcoming election. We were still working for Italy2, although the rumours were beginning to filter in that this move to Italy2 wasn't working as well as the Italians had hoped. Stories were coming in that in some of the other European plants, the maintenance was going back in-house.

Now, as much as I used to get the backroom lawyers telling me how crap it was working for Italy2, we'd never lost a penny. What New Holland achieved in a pay deal, we'd get. As far as I was concerned we had it good. We'd stayed in the pension scheme, so we were doing okay.

Michael Newman was a manager who would listen and I could do business with. Now Michael wasn't popular with a lot of the guys because he favoured his son Justin. Justin was an electrician and let's just say, he was looked after. Nepotism I think is the word I'm looking for.

It didn't bother me, it was something we all would do given the opportunity. But it got the backs up on a

few of the guys, and they'd regularly bend my ears about it. Jealousy, a terrible thing.
All the years Michael was my manager, I can only remember him losing his temper once. I can't remember the problem, something in my mind recalls we were organising a ballot. It was something Tony Lynch was trying to do and us three stewards wasn't having it. I should rephrase that. Eddie Priestaff and I weren't having it, the hoof was in his usual position of sitting on the fence.
Anyway, we were summoned to Michael's office to sort this problem out.
Michael had phoned me and said they were waiting for me. Now, always one to mix things up a bit I told him I was on my way. But I stopped at a vending machine and had a coffee.
Michael rang me again.
'Where are you?'
'I told you, I'm on my way.'
'Where you coming from ... Wickford?'
'Two minutes.' I told him. So, I waited for five and then walked in. Now the maintenance office was a rather large affair. With Michael's office at the far end. A row of desks was positioned for the various foreman. Trevor Evans, one of our foreman was sat at one. Nice guy and like me a Southend United supporter.
'Hurry up, they're waiting for you.' So, I knock and walk in. I'll set the scene. Michael behind his desk, glasses perched precariously at the end of his nose. Tony Lynch, one eye shut and gurning to one side. Eddie and the hoof sitting directly opposite Michael.

‘Where the fuck have you been?’ Asked Tony in his usual polite manner.
‘I have work to do, I can’t just drop everything because of you.’ I could see things were about to get lively, Tony didn’t like not getting his own way, and he didn’t like backchat. Michael seeing the tension rising tried to keep the meeting in an orderly fashion.
‘Now lads, what’s all this nonsense about?’ Well, what happened next has stayed with me forever. Eddie, a man of few words and gently spoken, looked across at Michael and said.
‘What the fucks it got to do with you.’ Well, it was if a powder keg had been lit, the room erupted. Michael, I’m not sure to this day what started him off, maybe he’d not been spoken to as a manager like that before. He stood up and threw his glasses at Eddie.
‘What’s it got to do with me, I’m your manager.’ All I can say is for the next five minutes the room was just full of shouting, pointing the finger, Tony and I set about each other, at one point I had to get between Eddie and Michael. I think I had Tony by the tie at some point. And through all this chaos sat the hoof, not saying anything, but getting whiter by the second. In the end, we were sent out, a calming down period was called for. The three of us walked out past a smiling Trevor Evans.
‘What time you meeting again? I’ll make sure I’m in here.’
We ended up going to Eddie’s electrical crib where we calmed down over a cup of tea. The hoof sat there pale and quiet. Things needed to be said.

'Hoof, you need to go. You are too old and gutless to be a steward.'
'I'm a year younger than Eddie.'
'You might be a year younger, but you're a liability, Trevor's right. You sat there like a tailor's dummy. You let us down.'
'But I don't like confrontation!' He hung himself. A shop steward who didn't like confrontation.

A few weeks later, he was booked in for an operation on the hoof. While he was away recuperating from that, they pensioned him off. Now, surprisingly for a man who never spent a penny without breaking into a sweat, he had bought a luxury caravan in the South of France. By doing that, it meant he would be gone a lot of the summer months. The munch was on board and I soon made him the branch chairman. I replaced hoof from the Labour Party chairman's position too. He was missing a lot of meetings with his new holiday home.
However, he still came to the branch meetings when he was home.

It was at a branch meeting that I read out an invitation to visit the European Parliament in Brussels. Obviously, you needed to be a Labour Party member and the trip included travelling there on the Eurostar and two nights in a hotel. The second evening would be a bit of a gala dinner with one of our MEP's.
The cost was sixty-nine pounds a head. We were a bit flush in the branch so I said if anybody at the meeting would like to go, the branch would pay.

Like the three amigos, hoof, munch and myself stepped forward.

If I thought the hotel business with Pat Brown couldn't be topped, I was in for a shock. The Pat Brown entertainment week was just a matinee for the main event.
I can only describe this trip as going on an excursion with Laurel and Harvey.
It all started well. I travelled with the hoof, and we met up with the munch at Waterloo. I spotted my two fellow committee members from the Eastern Region, Ford reps John and Les. Then we met the girl who is in charge of the trip and then the rest of the group. A mixed bunch to say the least. One, who I can't remember his name was a turban-wearing Geordie. Turned out to be a nice bloke, some older women and a couple of trainspotters and our little group that looked like the famous five. I'm guessing about twenty of us all told.
We had about forty minutes to kill before the train was due, so the five of us decided to get a refreshment. We hit the bar and the hoof did his normal hanging back approach. Munch stepped up, 'What do you want lads?' We order up a pint each and the hoof asked for a cup of tea.
I then read the hoof the riot act.
'Don't you embarrass me on this trip, you put your hand in your pocket.' The hoof did his usual innocent plea.

‘I was just about to ask but munch beat me to it.’ If dodging buying a beer was an Olympic sport, the hoof would have a whole collection of gold medals.
Munch returned with a tray with five pints.
‘Teas off, hoof.’
Just as we are finishing up, I tell the hoof to get a round in. Honestly, he was nearly in tears. The smile that came on his face as the trip organiser came in and said the train was in was unbelievable.
‘Oh, that’s a shame, I was just about to get you, boys, a drink.’

The trip on the train went quite quick. The four of us soon found the buffet car and the journey was, let’s say enjoyable. The hoof had hidden himself away somewhere, but to be honest I was past worrying about him. A coach picked us up at the train station and dropped us off at our hotel. It was late afternoon by the time we arrived.
Now, we had the evening to ourselves. John and Les had done this trip before and told us they knew a nice restaurant in town. So, we arranged to meet in the bar at seven and get a taxi to the restaurant. As per normal, the hoof did a swerve.
‘I’m going to eat in the hotel.’ He announced. Which most probably meant he’d done himself a packed lunch and would eat in his room. We went to our rooms and we were all on the same floor. The hoof was between munch and me.
I decided to grab a couple of hours and set the alarm on my phone for six-thirty.

After a power nap and a shower, I felt great. I head down to the bar just before seven and find the munch tucking into a beer and a large plate of chips?
'I'm starving,' he announced.
'But we're going out to eat in a minute.'
'Don't worry about that, this is just a starter.'
'Let's have a chip then,' I ask.
'Make sure it is one at this price.'
'Why, how much?'
'Seven euros.'
'What with the beer.'
'No seven euros for a plate of chips.'
I can't remember what the exchange rate was back then, but I think it's fair to say the munch had paid around five pounds for a plate of chips.
John and Les turned up with another guy from the group.
'Where's your mate, the hoof?'
'He didn't want to come, he's up in his room eating cheese sandwiches.' I joke.
'Yes, and watching the porn channel knowing him,' piped in the munch.
I must admit at that point I did think of Pat Brown and was hoping the hoof wasn't going to cause us a problem when checking out. I'd looked at the film channels and it came up that if you were on a pay per view channel for more than five minutes you would be charged for the whole film. Like the price of chips, it wasn't cheap.
We end up going in two taxis and after less than a ten-minute ride we arrive at a very nice-looking restaurant. Now, can I just state at this point, the

only other time I'd eaten out with the munch was at a McDonalds?

So, we go in and get a large table for the five of us. I sit opposite the munch and we order up. The beers come and we are in good spirits.

I suppose in the munch's defence, the menus were written in I believe Dutch and French, but unbeknown to me at that time, it was all Double-Dutch to the munch.

So, the food arrived. I had played it safe with a nice pate dish for starters. A huge bowl is placed in front of the munch.

'What you got there, mate?' I enquire.

'Soup.'

Now, I thought that was a wise choice for a skinny man who had tucked away a large plate of chips some thirty minutes earlier.

I start on my pate and toast and it was very nice. All of a sudden the munch spits out a large mouthful of soup.

'Aghhh,' he shouts out.

'What's up?'

'It's this soup, Trev. It's got fish in it.' He proceeds to chase a bit of fish around the bowl till he gets it on his spoon.

'Look.' Sure enough, sitting on his spoon was a fish head.

'Jesus Christ. What did you order?'

'Fish soup!!'

Now, I know we were in a different country, but I would imagine wherever you go in the world if you

order fish soup, there a strong possibility you might find fish in it.
Of course, this little pantomime scene had the others amused.
Next up, the main dish. I had ordered a chicken dish and very nice it looked too. The munch gets a large steak and salad plonked down in front of him.
'I don't believe it,' he moaned in his best Victor Meldrew voice.
'What's up now? That steak got meat in it?'
'No chips.' He called a waiter over and demanded chips.
'French fries, gracias.' I didn't like to tell him we were nowhere near Spain.
He picked at the steak and eventually gave me about three-quarters of it. Plus, most of his late delivery of chips.
A dessert trolley was wheeled around and he seemed to get a second wind. He picked two different desserts and made a right pig of himself. Washing it down with more beer, he started to look a little pale.

The Ford guys, past masters of pacing themselves were off to sample the nightlife. I looked at the state of the munch and thought I'd better get him back to the hotel.
We settle the bill and walk outside and hail a taxi. We were on the road about two minutes when he screams at the driver to stop. He jumps out and projectile vomits everywhere. Luckily not in the cab. However, the cab driver wouldn't let him back in and we ended up having to walk back to the hotel.

As we approached the entrance, we could see the hoof hovering about. He looked suspicious with his long coat and cloth cap on.
We crept up and tapped him on the shoulder.
'What are you up to?' He jumped out of his skin.
Then we saw what he was looking at. Across the road from the hotel was a few ladies of the night.
'Go to bed, Dave.' I suggested.

Next morning at breakfast we were told we had the morning to ourselves, then early afternoon we would be taken as a group to the European Parliament for a sit-in and a tour around, plus a chance to meet a few of our MEP's.
I think the three of us went for a walk around and ended up in a pizza place. We literally had to shake the hoof upside down by his ankles to get him to pay a third. In the afternoon, we were taken to the Parliament building and we sat in for an hour to listen in on a debate. We were given headphones and I take my hat off to the translators who could translate many different languages.
We ended up in a room with a couple of MEP's, neither had I heard of, then or since.
Once back at the hotel we were told to meet in one of the hotel function rooms where we would be wined and dined by one of our local MEP's, Richard Howitt.
I'd seen Richard a few times at Labour Party Conferences. To be honest I thought he was gay, however, he was married with kids, so I obviously got that wrong. He was a tall man, at least six feet six.

So, the high soft voice didn't quite go with the rest of him. The three of us sat at a table. The Ford guys decided they didn't want another night of Munch's eating disorder and kept away. There was a bottle of red and a bottle of white wine on the table. Hoof announced he only drank white wine. Munch and I weren't fussed as we stuck to the beer.

The evening was a bit of a bore, to be honest, Richard Howitt sat with us for at least five minutes before he wandered off.

By now hoof had sunk the white wine, but suddenly his statement of I only drink white wine wavered as his love of red wine had started? Might have had something to do with it being free.

So, after another hour, munch and I went off to the hotel bar. We had met two women from Ilford. Nothing in it, but we joined them and had a laugh. Later I'd gone up to the bar to get some more drinks and I looked out and spotted the hoof staggering in. Two bottles of wine were obviously taking its toll. In a language unbeknown to me, he ordered a drink. The barman surprisingly understood and put a large glass down which when I smelt I discovered was a neat whiskey.

'Easy Dave, we have to travel home in the morning.'

'Don't worry, I'm pacing myself.' Spotting munch, he staggered over and plonked himself down between the two women.

It was hard to understand him because he was slurring his words. Unfortunately, the women understood him only too well and next thing we knew

he'd got a slap. Munch pulled him up and sent him to bed.
After apologising for his behaviour, they settled down. A good hour must have passed and I was getting us a nightcap when I spotted hoof wandering around the foyer. I walked out to see what he was up to.
'What you doing?'
'I can't find my room?'
'Your room is between munch and mine.'
'I know, but where is that?'
'Wait here.' I go in and tell the others I'm calling it a night and go back and escort the hoof to his room. I shove him in and throw his key on his bed.
I get into my room, I'm feeling a bit drunk, but still knew what I was doing. I have a quick shower, drink a bottle of water, set my alarm for seven. We'd been told to be at breakfast for seven-thirty as we were being picked up at eight-thirty. It had just gone 2 am. I climbed into bed and within a minute I was drifting off.
A loud knocking on my door made me jump. I check my phone and its 3 am. I slip on my jeans and open the door. Standing there, swaying, was the hoof. In his hand, a TV remote.
'What the hell do you want?'
I've got my TV stuck on the porn channel and I can't switch it off. My batteries are dead. Can I borrow yours?'
'No.' I slammed the door.

As I get back into bed I can hear some shouting and gather hoof had woken the munch with the same request.

Next morning I'm woken by the alarm, I get showered and packed and enjoying a coffee before I go to breakfast. A sudden knocking on my door again made me jump. I open it and the munch is standing in just his Y-Fronts.

'Come on, we need to be at breakfast.'

'You going down like that, are you?' He looked down at himself and realised what a fool he looked.

'No, hang on.' He ran back to his room and within seconds he is back out in his jeans and t-shirt.

'Give the hoof a knock.' So, while munch is trying to get his shoes on I knock on the hoofs door.

I hear a groaning and eventually, the door is opened. I look through and can't see the hoof. I look down and there he is on all fours.

'Come on, breakfast time.'

'I don't feel well.'

'I'm not surprised. Two bottles of wine and a large whiskey. You need to get something down you, it will sort you out. You can't travel on an empty stomach.'

I can hear moaning in the background and as I walk in its coming from his TV.

'Bloody hell, you've still got the porn on.'

'I told you last night, I can't switch it off, my remotes not working.'

Munch walked over and pulled the plug.

'That was difficult, wasn't it.'

We end up wedging the hoof between us and escorting him down to the dining room. After getting him some tea and toast, I go and join the munch in getting Belgium's version of a full Monty breakfast. We're all sat around this big table.
The guy with the turban calls over to me in his broad Indian/Newcastle accent.
'Hey, Trev lad. Did you hear all that commotion outside our rooms last night?' Before I could answer, the munch stepped in. He didn't care that there were women at the table, he told them how it was. He pointed at the hoof.
'That would be this C***. Banging on my door asking if he could borrow my remote because he'd got the porn channel stuck on his TV.'
Well, you could have heard a pin drop. All eyes were on the hoof.
'I put it on by mistake.'
'Yes, he thought he watching a film called *Another Queen*. Turned out it was called *Anal Queens*,' wasn't it, hoof?'

Good old munch, never backwards coming forward. I never saw the hoof check out of the hotel, I would imagine he got stung heavily on his adult viewing. I half expected him to turn up at the next branch meeting and try and claim it back.

Chapter 11

Gone but never to be forgotten.

Well as we know, all good things must come to an end. I was summoned to Michael Newman's office and told the news. Our time with Italy2 was coming to an end. For me on a personal level I felt a bit sad, I thought we'd done well under this so-called maintenance specialist company. As for Michael, well I guess he knew the exit door wasn't far away. This is only my view on things, I might be completely off track here. I think Michael upset the hierarchy and once we were heading back a few scores were to be settled. One manager at the time, who I got to know, later on, was a very vindictive and nasty piece of work. I could imagine the frustration he had in not being able to get at Michael because we were with Italy2.

He never told me at that meeting, but I think we both knew it was the beginning of the end for him. He was in his mid-fifties at the time. But unfortunately, his days were numbered.

The *rat* phoned me, he couldn't wait to tell me the news. I went to see him. Now, because he was so unpopular, he'd moved the convenors office out of the factory and into the Admin building.

Have you ever heard of such a thing? An hourly paid convenor that was based away from the factory.

I'd not seen him for a long time. He'd rarely be seen on the shop floor.

I knew he wanted to see me and gloat. Plus of course, he was still angry that I'd changed from the Transport and General union to the AEEU, or Amicus as we were now called.

Now, this chapter is going to be very difficult to put any humour in. This was the time of big change.
As I went into the convenors office I was surprised to see how bloated and ill he looked. Ridiculous comes to mind when I think back to how he looked as he sat there.
Bloated, puffy faced, pale and dyed hair. Here was a man who had a heart attack in his early thirties, smoked like a trouper and did no exercise. How is he still alive? I have a message for him. Keep moving *rat* before they start throwing dirt over you.
Any respect I had for this man had long gone. I knew what he'd been up to. Things had happened in the plant that was a disgrace. But we'll come to all that shortly.
What I remember it was the briefest of meetings with him. He told me nothing that I didn't already know. I knew I'd always remain a junior steward now. I wasn't Transport and General anymore, so all the plum roles would stay with them.
I didn't care, I was doing well without all that crap. I was a branch secretary, a member of the Amicus Eastern Region executive committee and the secretary of the local Labour Party, plus I'd recently been put onto the Amicus political committee which guaranteed a place at the Labour Party conference each year. All these positions were untouchable to

the likes of the *rat* and the Transport and General stewards.
I should mention at this point that the rest of the guys I got on well with. The likes of Geoffrey Martin-Smith, Alan Phillips, Paul Norris and a new steward, Warren Gibson, I think I can say we had a healthy respect for each other. I knew they would always stick together, but I think they were happy to have their numbers bolstered a bit.

Before the transfer back to the company happened, a major shock was announced. The *rat* had gone. Rumours were rife, but to be fair to the remaining T&G stewards, they kept a lid on the reason for his sudden departure.
I knew something must have happened because he wouldn't have gone voluntarily. The *rat* would have been around the fifty-five mark when this happened.
I recently contacted Warren Gibson who I knew would tell me the truth in the reason of the *rat's* departure. He was more than happy to put the record straight.
I'd suspected for years he was on the take one way or another. The way he rolled over on letting contractors take the work away from our men, was a disgrace. I could fill this book up with his dodgy deals

The security takeover was downright criminal. That was the straw that broke the camel's back when that happened. As I mentioned earlier in the book, I couldn't be party to that, so I resigned.

So, Warren told me exactly what happened, and I will use the word **allegedly** happened to save any comebacks.
It was the time when the *rat* had bought the bungalow in Benfleet. The bungalow Tony Lynch was trying to find when we played *follow the van*.
Now the *rat* obviously had a lot of power, so he got a few of the stewards to help him move some stuff from his house in Canvey Island to Benfleet, during working time.
His laziness and abuse of power led to his downfall. Warren and two other stewards who I won't name were removing contents from the house when they came across a tin of old payslips. A lot of them unopened. Curiosity and the mistrust they must have felt at the time led them to open a fairly recent payslip.
What they found was incredible. **Allegedly** the payslip showed that the *rat* was no longer hourly paid, but paid as a staff member. They worked out that the monthly rate he was on was around what a manager would expect to be paid.
Could this scandalous accusation be true?
Well, I'll never really know, I wasn't there. If it is true, then it all makes sense. The outsourcing, the cowboy type of firms that were coming in. The poor results of pay negotiations. If it is true, my god the H/R personnel at the time must have been rubbing their hands together. They had the convenor in their pocket.
Warren has no reason to lie about what **allegedly** happened.

Two things I will say about this. It brings me back to the way a convenor is chosen in the plant. It's badly floored when a convenor is protected and doesn't have to face the membership. No way would the **alleged** activities of that man happen if he had to rely on the workforce to get re-elected.

A few of the stewards who were long-time supporters of the *rat* should be hanging their heads in shame for letting it continue for so many years. I won't name you, but you know who you are.

Unlike the previous convenor, George Catton, who took the underhand way he was removed like a true gentleman. The *rat*, true to his nickname, scurried away to count his money. Too embarrassed to ever show his face back at the plant again.

I've been told that he tried to get support by saying he'd never let these company incentives affect is work as the convenor. Thank god, the rest of the stewards had some

backbone and shipped him out. So, there he is, some fifteen years later, still living off a manager's pension. Bloody disgraceful.

Let's not waste any more ink on that pathetic excuse of a human being.

Chapter 12

New Beginnings

Out with the old and in with the new. Well, not new by any stretch of the imagination.
Enter Geoffrey Martin-Smith as the new convenor.
At the time, I would think Geoff had been a shop steward for a good thirty years. I have to admit I wasn't a huge fan of Geoff in his early years as a convenor. But since my recent discovery of the man he took over from, I have nothing but admiration for the guy.
He had to take over and inherit all the shit deals the *rat* had agreed to over many years.
All this happened while we were at the dregs at our time with Italy2.
Things happened fast when we did come back in-house. As predicted, Michael Newman was soon shown the door, along with a few of our foreman, including the notorious Tony Lynch. Eddie Priestaff called it a day and left just the munch and me to come back in the fold as stewards.
We had a new manager appointed, Philip Harris. Strange choice, Phil had progressed from the tools to an engineer and was now promoted to take care of the maintenance. We were a sinking entity; the engine side of the business was disappearing fast. Within eighteen months one whole side of the factory was empty. Now, Phil looked like a choirboy, and to be fair to the guy he was in my eyes a decent enough manager.

However, his boss was a different kettle of fish. I was now faced with a man who made my old manager from way back, Bambini look like a saint. Tough times were coming for the guys in maintenance.
Enter *Bill Sikes.*
I'll come to this piece of work later.

I must admit I was in for a bit of a shock when I joined up with the old stewards. I'm not sure how long it had been since I was last with them as a steward. I'd resigned when the security was taken over by Wyatt Earp and his gang. Add on to that the three years with Italy2, it must have been a good decade.
To be honest, I wasn't prepared for the shock of seeing how things had slipped.
Gone were any scheduled meetings with the company. There was no such thing as a Joint Works Committee. Shop steward's meetings were ad hoc and not minutes were taken. There were no records kept. To be honest, he convenors office looked like it had been burgled.
I don't know, but I guess it suited the *rat*, after all, he'd removed the office out to the back and beyond.
Unfortunately, Geoff was happy to let it continue. Of course, once you let things go like that, the company would never let you get them back.
What a turnaround, from the days of Bill Cleary and George Catton. Everything was organised, the meetings were set in stone, minutes of the meetings would come out on the factory floor at regular intervals. The guys were kept informed.

The stewards held some respect back then. I do remember bringing it up with Geoff and Warren who was then the vice-convenor.
They did hold their hands up with embarrassment, but nothing changed. Such a shame.

It didn't take long for the maintenance moaners who were regularly berating me about how bad it was working for Italy2, to be singing a different tune.
They started loaning us maintenance guys to production. If an area was short, we'd be obliged to send two or three guys over to work on the line. It was tough, it's not easy work, and if you've only done maintenance work for thirty years, trying to keep up with a moving assembly line wasn't an easy task.
I can remember being loaned myself with a fitter named Andy Sackett.
Christ, that was a long week. We'd been given the job of putting the steps on, we couldn't believe it when the guy showing us said we were doing a job that one man normally did.
We thought we had it sussed one morning, we didn't do every tractor, some didn't have the steps we were fitting. Andy walked up the line and returned smiling.
'Stand down, we have a gap of ten tractors.'
In theory, I worked out that we had a good thirty to forty minutes plus to relax.
'I'm going for a poo,' I announced. Luckily the toilets are next to the line, so I go in and relax with my paper. Just as I'm finishing off I get Andy shouting at me through the door.

‘Hurry up, I got it wrong, we’ve missed a couple.’ My god, I came out and we were now in the shit, literally. We had to chase down the line and for a good hour do our best to catch up. I think I lost half a stone that week. Better than any slimming club.

If work was getting more difficult, I was at least enjoying my time away at different facets of the union. I was attending many conferences. I’d somehow got myself an invite to the TUC conference. Now I was there representing the Amicus motor vehicles executive committee. I was asked to do a 3-minute speech on the decline of the UK motor industry. So basically, apart from this 3 minutes, I had five days to relax and enjoy the conference, and of course, in the evenings do some networking over a few beers. I was put into a nice hotel in Brighton and was having the time of my life.

On the Thursday, I was due to speak. Now people who know me will vouch that this is something I don’t have any trouble with.

I reported to the administrator’s office first thing and they gave me a beeper. My instructions were simple, when your beeper goes off, report to the side of the stage. Show them your ID, and they will tell you what to do. What could possibly go wrong?

I had my speech in my pocket and was looking forward to delivering a damning account on how the motor vehicle industry was in a downward spiral. I’d done my research, timed the speech and was feeling confident.

That morning I was listening to various speakers and suddenly the bleep vibrated in my pocket. It made me jump and suddenly I was feeling a tad nervous. I made my way to the side of the stage and produced my ID.

I was told to wait until the next person stood up to speak. Then go and sit on the side of the stage. So, I waited, and as soon as the next speaker made his way to the lectern, I made my way up.

Now, there was a man already sitting there who was obviously next to go, I sat down next to him and I could feel the shaking coming from him.

'Nervous?' I enquire.

'Bricking it, mate. I've never done anything like this before. And that doesn't help.'

When I looked at where he was pointing I could see a huge screen staring at you from the stage. So, as you spoke, you could see a giant headshot of yourself.

'I see what you mean. I bet he's regretting eating a black seeded roll for lunch.'

That little funny from me settled the guy down a bit.

A thirty-second warning beep could be heard and the guy on the stage closed his speech.

'Fancy a beer after?' He asked.

'Go on then, I'll see you in the Aussie bar next-door.'

I can't remember his name, but I didn't make the bar for a drink. For as he walked out onto the stage, the man behind me sat down. Not any man, the bloody Prime Minister. Yes, Gordon Brown had plonked himself down. Not knowing the correct etiquette, I just hit him with, 'Alright Gordon.'

To be fair he said hello back, and I was now keen to show off my hard-hitting but with a touch of humour speech.

I think the nerves were beginning to get to me, which caused me to keep talking. I don't know what I was rambling on about, but it drew attention to Gordon's bodyguard who I could see staring at me from the side of the stage. He gave me the two-finger gesture, not the one that you stick up, the one where you point to your own eyes and then to the other person. It was his way of saying "I'm watching you and shut the fuck up." Next thing I'm being tapped on the shoulder.

'Excuse me, Mr Whitehead, do you mind waiting. We want Gordon to go on next.' Some flunky had put paid to my five minutes of fame. I was angry, so said back.

'Of course, no problem.' Well, what else could I say?

Now Gordon Brown wasn't my cup of tea I have to say. His popularity was on the slide at that time. But one thing he could do, he could deliver a great speech. So, for ninety minutes, I sat and listened, and started to sweat. Not helped by the bodyguard still scouring at me. Imagine what it feels like when you've been persuaded to get up and sing at a karaoke night. You can't really sing, but you'll give it a go. Suddenly a guy gets up and sounds like Frank Sinatra. You pray and hope, but to no avail, your name is called out to follow that guy.

So, by the time Gordon had finished, all my confidence and self-belief in myself had long gone. In

fact, I was becoming a jabbering wreck. Gordon walked off to sumptuous applause. I stood up, walked out to the lectern and pulled my speech out of my pocket, and it was if I'd used invisible ink? The ink had disappeared in my sweaty pocket.
'What the fuck.' Maybe not the greatest opening line of any speech, but a certain attention grabber. I'd forgotten about the microphone and my deep voice was now booming across the auditorium. If any of the delegates weren't paying much attention, they certainly were now. I looked up and could see my giant head staring back at me.
'He's got a cheek that Gordon, making me wait ninety minutes to come out here. Some bugger has nicked my ink off my notes while I've been waiting.' I held my blank paper up and got a laugh.
To this day I couldn't tell you what I spoke about for the three minutes. Obviously, I must have somehow mentioned the motor industry, but trust me when I say that I must have waffled on and was praying for the thirty-second warning beep. I think I was mediocre to poor, judging by the limp applause at the end.
Funny enough, I was never asked to talk at a conference again? Not sure why.

I preferred the Labour Party Conferences, I built up friendships with guys that I still have contact with today.
For some reason, the Welsh contingent took a liking to me. I'd go out and have a drink with them at night and they were great fun.

They smuggled me into their gala evening, it was in some hotel and they had a spare pass as one of their group hadn't made to the conference.

'You need to get rid of that cockney accent, Trev and try and speak a bit Welsh sounding.' Sound advice from one of their group. Well, that was no problem to me boyo.

I had a great night, got drunk and ended up dancing with Glenys Kinnock. The only Englishman amongst a thousand Welsh, what a night.

My last Labour Party Conference was in Manchester in 2008. They saved the best till last. It started off bad as I never received my invite. I was going as part of the Amicus trade union delegation. Someone had dropped a clanger and left me off. So, after contacting the union I received a very apologetic phone call from a woman from the Trade Union. Now, because it was late in the day, all the hotels were booked up. The only one with rooms was the Hilton, and it wasn't a room, it was a suite. I didn't know this until I arrived. I took the train to Manchester and strolled into this very impressive hotel. After a thorough body search by two rather large men. I went into the lobby. I stood in a queue waiting to book in. A very nice young lady asked to see my booking details.

'Oh,' She looked at me with a tad of amazement.

'Your VIP, you don't need to queue, come with me.'

She led me to a very plush lounge area and I got booked in.

'I'll take you to your room,' she announced. We go over to a lift that has emblazoned, VIP guests only.

This lift I found out later was manned 24/7. So, we go up to the one from the top floor and I enter the world of the rich. God knows what this suite cost a night, but we're talking serious money I would imagine.
It was floor to ceiling glass. A lounge, a bedroom with an eight-foot bed. A bathroom with everything including one of those showers that squirts you everywhere and a huge jacuzzi bath.
I then get taken up a floor where I'm shown a lounge area reserved for VIP guests. I was informed that this lounge was open from 11 am to 7 pm. Now here's the thing, this lounge had food, beer, wine, all sorts. I had to endure this treatment for five days.
Now if I didn't think things could get any better, the following morning I came out of my room at the same time as my new next-door neighbour. Old Mr 2 Jags himself, John Prescott. I introduced myself and we shook hands.
And what a nice bloke he turned out to be. We went down for breakfast together and he asked me to join him. He was on the way out at this time, he'd been Deputy Prime Minister but he was getting past his sell-by date. Although he had a Yorkshire accent, he was in fact, Welsh. He was funny and amusing and had a real dry wit about him.
He didn't suffer fools gladly and he had me in stitches with his antics. He had the waiter running around for him, and one incident that first morning sticks in my mind. Some guy in a very smart suit came over to our table.
'Good morning John, my secretary phoned me and said you wanted to speak to me urgently.'

'Not now, Richard. Can you not see I'm having my breakfast?'
'Oh .... Sorry, John. I'll wait in reception.' The guy walked off and John waited for him to disappear and then pulled his phone out of his pocket. Putting on a thick set of reading glasses he played with the phone and then stuck it to his ear.
'Hello, Sylvia. What the hell did I ring you about this morning? I had Richard here just now saying I wanted to speak to him urgently?' Smiling at me he listened.
'That's it, for the life of me I couldn't think what it was.' Putting his phone back in his pocket he looked at me and said something my dad would often say.
'No fun getting old, Trevor.'

The conferences were a time to make new contacts and do what is known as a bit of networking. It was also an excuse to get bladdered every night. The hoof would have fitted in well because if you were that way inclined, you could get into most functions and grab a few free drinks. My other Amicus colleagues were in modest accommodation, and I didn't feel the need to brag about my VIP upgrade. After conference finished for the day, we would normally have a couple of drinks before going back to our respected hotels. Maybe with an arrangement to go to some function or another. Obviously, I was keen to spend a couple of hours hobnobbing in my VIP freebie lounge. Unfortunately, John Prescott blew my cover one night. A few of us had gone to some function, we came out slightly worse for wear. Now

because of the high level of security, there was never any danger to you. Everywhere you looked you'd see armed police. As long as you had you ID hanging from your neck, you were fine.
We were walking back in the direction of our respected hotels when one of my colleagues pointed across the road.
'Isn't that John Prescott over there?' Indeed, it was, and he was being surrounded by some young girls who were trying to get a photo with him. All of a sudden his bellowing voice boomed our way.
'Trev, come over here and take a photo will you lad?'
'You know John Prescott?' One of my colleagues asked.
'Err ... Sort of.' I mumbled as I walked over. A girl gave me her camera and I took various photos of these girls hanging off John. Eventually, they walked off.
'Not bad for seventy, am I lad? Come on I'll walk back to the hotel with you.'
I said goodnight to my colleagues and knew I would be getting an inquisition in the morning.
Now I should say that we went back straight to the hotel, but John had a lot of stamina for a seventy-year-old and he took me to a certain kind of club. I'll park that story there and save the rest for my memoirs.

I have hundreds of stories about my conference experiences, I met loads of nice people, many so-called celebrities. My favourite, Kate Garraway, odd choice maybe, but I really liked her. It was soon after her exploits on Strictly Come Dancing. She was lovely and really down to earth. Chatted away to me, so much nicer than the ginger minge from Eastenders. But this book is really about the factory, so let's get back to work.

It seemed every few weeks *Bill Sikes* would call me to his office and give me more bad news. Look, I don't want to be unkind to the man. The end of the day, it was the nature of the beast. He was being told to cut down on the headcount, and that had to happen. I could sit with him all day and argue the case for keeping our guys, but it wouldn't make any difference.
It didn't win him any polls on the popularity charts. In fact, even to this day, I can't find anyone who has a good word to say about him.
Of course, a new tool had been introduced along with the thousands of other politically correct changes. Since year dot the way we would lose people was by the last in, first out rule. But now, thanks to a new system called Matrix. That rule was no longer applied. In fact, it became illegal to use.
You were discriminating against someone for not having long service? Absolute bullshit and madness. So basically, the manager would give you points for all sorts of skills and attitude.
It's in my mind completely flawed. If your face didn't fit, it was good night Eileen.
The company were doing nothing wrong, they were abiding by the laws that were now in place.

But it was hard to explain to a guy with thirty years' service that your surplus to requirements and no longer needed.

It was an awful time, and I dreaded the phone call from *Bill Sikes*, it was never going to be good news. I had to sit there and watch him destroy people's lives. For me, well I thought everything was going to shit. I know the maintenance guys were fed up with me and the munch. But there was nothing we could do. Trust me, had the munch and me not been stewards at the time, I'm certain we would have both been shipped out. On the union front, Amicus were in a merger with the T & G. I was going back to my roots. Unfortunately, the T & G had a much larger membership, so I knew my time on any union executive committee was not going to last much longer. We became UNITE. And within a year I'd lost all my former amicus positions apart from carrying on as the branch secretary.
The shop stewards in the plant were down to a handful. We had become a laughing stock, I'm not going to point out the blame, they'd let things slip to such an extinct that we had no support. Warren Gibson had gone. If we had a mass meeting to discuss a pay deal, I could see the real anger in the guys. The respect had gone and we were targeted to some real abuse. How Geoff kept a level head at these meetings I'll never know. Sometimes I was worried about his safety as the meeting got really heated and threatened to boil over. All sorts of

accusations and abuse were thrown at us. We were literally hated by the majority of the membership.

I was fifty-four and I'd had enough. In the space of a year, everything had worn me down. The constant looking at shrinking the maintenance headcount. We'd lost a huge amount of hoist work due to the engine side closing. The Health and Safety rules that made our life so difficult. It wasn't fun anymore. Phillip Harris was another casualty, replaced by a former contractor.
As I mentioned earlier, I knew *Bill Sikes* was keen to ship me out, it must have been very frustrating for him as I was protected by my shop steward status.

In the end, I jumped before I was pushed. It was 2010 and it was game over. I left the company. Within a week I was on a plane bound for Asia. I've never returned.

Authors summary

As I started this book it occurred to me that it wasn't ethical to name the company, or I should say companies that were and are now associated with the plant. So, I did my best to semi-disguise them.
I did keep to the majority of true names. Munch and the Hoof are nicknames associated with the pair of them. *Bill Sikes,* I decided not to reveal his real name. He is a nasty piece of work who got real enjoyment in picking certain people off. Not sure what his problem was, maybe he was bullied as a youngster. As mentioned in the book, I couldn't find one person who had a good word to say about him. The ex-convenor I named the *rat*. Mainly because that is what he was, so absolutely the right name for him. I did fear if I used his real name it could lead to some safety concerns. Some people have long memories. Some guys will be disappointed they are not mentioned, along with guys who wished they weren't.
Geoff gave me numerous stories, unfortunately, many I couldn't use in respect of their families. Warren gave me a lot more on the *rat*, but I decided enough was said about him.
A couple of close colleagues and friends passed away this year.
Richard Llewellyn and Brian Crease. Both of similar age to me, so without sounding like a Paul Norris quote, I thought it would be a good time to get some of the antics into print.

To the guys that are mentioned, I hope you don't mind. Look on the Brightside, you'll forever be named in print as a copy of this book will be stored in the British Library. To those I protected by disguising your name, think yourself lucky. You may not be so lucky if I decide to write a part two.
To people who read this book and have never stepped foot in the factory, well I hope you enjoyed the stories. I had a hell of a time in over thirty years working at the plant.

If you enjoyed the book and like my style of humorous writing, I hope you try some of my other books. I can recommend the Arthur Ascot trilogy. I have received many positive reviews for that series of books.

I'd also welcome any feedback, feel free to email me.
trevorwhitehead58@gmail.com

Also by this author:

The Curry Affect
Arthur Ascot PI
Ascot & Plunkett
The UK's Number 1 Private Investigation Agency
Pattaya Dangerous

All available on Amazon.
Trevor Whitehead's authors page:
https://www.amazon.com/Trevor-Whitehead/e/B01N5NNZ3E

24731242R00132

Printed in Great Britain
by Amazon